I0800866

BLACK SLAVERY IN THE MARITIMES

THE **BROADVIEW SOURCES** SERIES

Black Slavery in the Maritimes

A HISTORY IN DOCUMENTS

edited by HARVEY AMANI WHITFIELD

broadview press

BROADVIEW PRESS – www.broadviewpress.com
Peterborough, Ontario, Canada

Founded in 1985, Broadview Press remains a wholly independent publishing house. Broadview's focus is on academic publishing; our titles are accessible to university and college students as well as scholars and general readers. With over 600 titles in print, Broadview has become a leading international publisher in the humanities, with world-wide distribution. Broadview is committed to environmentally responsible publishing and fair business practices.

Library and Archives Canada Cataloguing in Publication

Black slavery in the Maritimes : a history in documents / edited by Harvey Amani Whitfield.

(The Broadview sources series)
Includes bibliographical references.
ISBN 978-1-55481-386-5 (softcover)

1. Slavery—Maritime Provinces—History—Sources. 2. Slaves—Maritime Provinces—History—Sources. 3. Black Canadians—Maritime Provinces—History—Sources. 4. Blacks—Maritime Provinces—History—Sources. I. Whitfield, Harvey Amani, 1974-, editor II. Series: Broadview sources series

HT1052.M37B53 2018 306.3'6209715 C2018-901759-7

Broadview Press handles its own distribution in North America:
PO Box 1243, Peterborough, Ontario K9J 7H5, Canada
555 Riverwalk Parkway, Tonawanda, NY 14150, USA
Tel: (705) 743-8990; Fax: (705) 743-8353
email: customerservice@broadviewpress.com

Distribution is handled by Eurospan Group in the UK, Europe, Central Asia, Middle East, Africa, India, Southeast Asia, Central America, South America, and the Caribbean. Distribution is handled by Footprint Books in Australia and New Zealand.

Canada Broadview Press acknowledges the financial support of the Government of Canada through the Canada Book Fund for our publishing activities.

Copy-edited by Juliet Sutcliffe
Book Design by Em Dash Design

PRINTED IN CANADA

CONTENTS

Acknowledgements ix
Introduction 1
Chronology 19
Questions to Consider 21

PART I: RUNAWAY SLAVE ADVERTISEMENTS AND SLAVE FOR SALE NOTICES 23

1. Halifax Slaves for Sale in Boston, Massachusetts (1751) 24
2. Slaves for Sale, Halifax, Nova Scotia (1752) 25
3. Runaway Slave Advertisement, Female Slave Named Thursday, Nova Scotia (1772) 26
4. Slave Wanted Advertisement, Nova Scotia (1776) 28
5. Female Slave to Be Sold at Public Auction, Nova Scotia (1783) 29
6. Runaway Advertisement, James, Nova Scotia (1781 and 1786) 30
7. Runaway Slave Advertisement, An African Slave, Nova Scotia (1783) 32
8. Runaway Slave Advertisement, Dick, Nova Scotia (1783) 33
9. Runaway Slave Advertisement, Ben, Nova Scotia (1783) 34
10. Slave for Sale, "Negro Boy," New Brunswick (1784) 35
11. Runaway Slave Advertisement, Hector, New Brunswick (1784) 36
12. Runaway Advertisement, Unfree Black Laborers, New Brunswick (1784) 37
13. Runaway Slave Advertisement, Jupiter and Clarinda, Nova Scotia (1784) 41
14. A Family Escapes, Nova Scotia (1785) 42
15. Slave for Sale Advertisement, 14-Year-Old, Nova Scotia (1786) 43
16. Slave for Sale Advertisement, 14-Year-Old Boy, New Brunswick (1786) 44
17. Slaves for Sale Advertisement, A Man and Boy, New Brunswick (1786) 45
18. Runaway Slave Advertisement, Ben, New Brunswick (1786) 46
19. Runaway Slave Advertisement, Five Slaves Escape Caleb Jones, New Brunswick (1786) 47
20. Runaway Slave Advertisement, Dinah, Nova Scotia (1786) 48
21. Slave for Sale Advertisement, Teenage Girl, New Brunswick (1787) 49
22. Slave for Sale Advertisement, Young Woman, New Brunswick (1787) 50
23. Runaway Slave Advertisement, Sam and Beller (siblings) Escape, New Brunswick (1787) 51
24. Runaway Slave Advertisement, Abraham, Teenager, New Brunswick (1787) 52

25. Runaway Slave Advertisement, London, Age 18, New Brunswick (1787) 53
26. Runaway Slave Advertisement, Keziah, New Brunswick (1787) 54
27. Slave for Sale Advertisement, Young Black Woman, New Brunswick (1788) 55
28. Runaway Slave Advertisement, Prince, New Brunswick (1788) 56
29. Runaway Slave Advertisement, Poll, New Brunswick (1791) 57
30. Runaway Slave Advertisement, Statia and Her Family, New Brunswick (1792) 58
31. Runaway Slave Advertisement, Prince, New Brunswick (1792) 60
32. Runaway Slave Advertisement, Joseph Odel and Peter Lawrence, Nova Scotia (1792) 61
33. Runaway Slave Advertisement, Bill/Belfast, Nova Scotia (1794) 62
34. Slave for Sale, Young Man, New Brunswick (1799) 64
35. Runaway Slave Advertisement, Gill and Dick, New Brunswick (1799) 65
36. Female Sold for a Term of Years, Nova Scotia (1800) 66
37. Runaway Slave Advertisement, Two Slaves, New Brunswick (1802) 67
38. Runaway Slave Advertisement, Dinah, New Brunswick (1806) 68
39. Slave for Sale, Nancy, New Brunswick (1809) 69
40. Runaway Slave Advertisement, Lidge Escapes Again, New Brunswick (1816) 70
41. Runaway Advertisement, Samuel Hutchings, New Brunswick (1818) 71

PART II: LETTERS, NARRATIVES, NEWSPAPERS, PETITIONS 73

42. John Wentworth Letter about His 19 Slaves, Nova Scotia (1784) 74
43. Petition of Zimri Armstrong about Re-enslavement, New Brunswick (1785) 76
44. James MacGregor, A Letter to a *Clergyman Urging him to set free a Black Girl he held in SLAVERY*, Nova Scotia (1788) 78
45. Petition of Thomas Peters to the British Government (1790) 79
46. John Clarkson's Diary, Lydia Jackson's Re-enslavement and Other Observations (1791) 81
47. Thomas Clarkson, "Some Account of the New Colony at Sierra Leone," Re-enslavement (1792) 84
48. David George's Narrative (1793) 86
49. Boston King's Narrative (1798) 87

50. Gradual Emancipation of Jack and Amelia in Prince Edward Island (1800) 89
51. Joseph Aplin's Racial Justification for Slavery (1801) 91
52. Excerpts from *Opinions of Several Gentlemen of the Law, on the Subject of Negro Servitude in the Province of Nova-Scotia* (1802) 92
53. Digby Slave-Owners' Petition, Nova Scotia (1807) 93
54. Petition of Isaac Willoughby, Former Slave, Nova Scotia (1834) 97
55. Article Supporting Slavery and Decrying Free Blacks, Nova Scotia (1842) 99

PART III: COURT CASES AND BILLS OF SALE 101

56. Bill of Sale, Young Boy from Maryland, Nova Scotia (1779) 103
57. Bill of Sale, Mintur (1779) 104
58. *R. v. Jesse Gray*, for Whipping Pero 100 Times, Nova Scotia (1786) 106
59. Mary Postell Affidavit, Nova Scotia (1791) 107
60. Grand Jury Complaint, Re-enslavement of Black Boy Sent to the West Indies Illegally, Nova Scotia (1794) 110
61. James DeLancey Complaint Against William Woodin (1803) 112
62. Supreme Court Case "Nancy," New Brunswick (1800) 114
63. Ward Chipman's Slavery Brief, New Brunswick Supreme Court (1800) 115
64. *R. v. Andrews* (Indictment of Samuel Andrews Jr.), Slave-Owners Murder a Female Slave, Yarmouth, Nova Scotia (1801) 116
65. Slave Returned to Owner, Supreme Court, Prince Edward Island (1802) 117
66. Bill of Sale for Percilla, Eight-Year-Old Girl, Nova Scotia (1804) 118
67. Supreme Court Case, Newspaper Account, New Brunswick (1806) 119

PART IV: GOVERNMENT DOCUMENTS 123

68. Governor Cornwallis Discusses Captain Bloss and His Slaves (1750) 124
69. An Act, *declaring that* Baptism *of* SLAVES *shall not exempt them from* BONDAGE, Prince Edward Island (1781) 125
70. Book of Negroes 126
71. Dick Hill, Re-Enslaved, Shelburne, Nova Scotia (1787) 128
72. An Act for the Regulation & Relief of the Free Negroes within the Province of Nova Scotia (Unpassed) (1789) 129
73. A Bill Relating to Negroes (Unpassed), New Brunswick (6 February 1801) 131

74. AN ACT *to repeal an Act made and passed in the twenty-first year of his late Majesty's reign intituled* "An Act, *declaring that* Baptism *of* SLAVES *shall not exempt them from* BONDAGE," Prince Edward Island (1825) 132

75. Prince Edward Island and Montserrat Connection (1828) 133

PART V: WILLS AND CHURCH RECORDS 135

76. Will of Joseph Totten, Nova Scotia (1788) 136

77. Will of Thomas Leonard, Nova Scotia (1788) 138

78. Will of Anna Lillie (or Ann Lilie), Nova Scotia (1789) 139

79. Teenage Slave Diana Bastian Burial Note—Her Rape and Pregnancy by George More, Member of Council, Cape Breton (1792) 140

80. Will of Caleb Fowler, Nova Scotia (1793) 141

81. Will of George Cornwall, Nova Scotia (1799) 142

82. Will of Jacob Ellegood, New Brunswick (1802) 143

83. Will of Benjamin Belcher, Nova Scotia (1801) 144

84. Will of Jacob Troop, Nova Scotia (1805) 146

85. Will of Isaac Bonnell, Nova Scotia (1806) 147

86. Will of William Wanton, New Brunswick (1812) 148

87. Will of William Schurman, Prince Edward Island (1819) 149

Suggested Readings 151

ACKNOWLEDGEMENTS

I am thankful to the Department of History at the University of Vermont for its generous financial support. I would like to thank my research assistants, Jesse Eaton and Franco Paz, for their wonderful support during this project. I owe many intellectual debts to various scholars including T.H. Breen, Alan Taylor, Paul Lovejoy, Ruma Chopra, Sean Field, Erik Esselstrom, Sarah Osten, and many others. I am particularly thankful to my dear friend Krista Kesselring for suggesting this project to me one evening in Halifax. Stephen Latta and Juliet Sutcliffe have been supportive and patient editors. I am truly blessed to have enjoyed the support of my wife Natalie and young daughter Hope.

INTRODUCTION[1]

The introduction and development of slavery in the New World is among the most important events in global history, resulting in the growth of a lucrative and exploitative labour system justified by perceived racial differences. Slavery existed throughout the New World, from Chile and Argentina in the south to Nova Scotia in the north. It is not surprising that slavery played a part in Canadian history, but it is startling that it has not received widespread attention from the general Canadian public and historians alike.[2] Slavery is the most neglected aspect of pre-Confederation Canadian history. The focus, understandably, when discussing African Canadian history has been on the Underground Railroad, the **Black Loyalists**, and other groups who found freedom under the British flag. Yet thousands of black people were enslaved in the Maritimes, Quebec, and Upper Canada between the seventeenth and early nineteenth centuries (1605–1820s). This sourcebook offers readers an opportunity to explore the contours of black slavery in the Maritimes, and invites them to consider how it might affect their broader understanding of Canadian and American history.[3] This introduction summarizes the major events and themes of slavery in Nova Scotia, New Brunswick, and Prince Edward Island.

Black Loyalists: African Americans who took advantage of British military proclamations offering freedom to slaves of American patriots if they left their owners and came to British lines. The Black Loyalists performed numerous duties for the British forces ranging from much-needed manual labour to actual fighting.

BLACK MIGRATION AND THE ORIGINS OF MARITIME SLAVERY

Black migration is one of the hallmarks of the history of the Maritimes. These migrations—coerced and voluntary—connected the Maritimes to the United States, Africa, the Caribbean, and Europe. Between 1605 and 1820, several thousand black people settled in the Maritimes. These migrants included 3,000 Black Loyalists, 1,500 to 2,000 Loyalist slaves, 550 **Jamaican Maroons** (from 1796 to 1800) several hundred slaves in Île Royale, an unknown number of New England Planter slaves (possibly up to 200), a small number of slaves brought up from the coastal slave trade (Documents

Jamaican Maroons: In 1796, the Jamaican government deported approximately 550 Trelawney Town Maroons to Nova Scotia. They were deported because, in the midst of the Saint-Domingue Rebellion, Jamaican planters viewed them as threatening to the stability of the slave regime in Jamaica. They remained in Nova Scotia for only four years before nearly all of them left for Sierra Leone.

1 Some passages from this book's Introduction are excerpted from the editor's previous work. Excerpts reprinted with permission of the Publisher from *North to Bondage* by Harvey Amani Whitfield © University of British Columbia Press 2016. All rights reserved by the publisher.

2 See Suggested Readings, p. 151.

3 Aboriginal slavery is an extraordinarily important aspect of Canadian history, and one that deserves a separate volume. Quebec and Ontario, with their significant history of Aboriginal slavery, would also benefit from a documentary history that focuses on those regions. The Maritimes is unique in terms of the numbers of black people, both coerced and voluntary, who migrated there between 1700 and 1820 including the French slaves in Île Royale, New England Planter slaves, Black Loyalists, Loyalist slaves, Jamaican Maroons, and black refugees from the War of 1812.

1 and 2, pp. 24 and 25), and about 3,200 Black refugees from the War of 1812.[4] We must understand the history of slavery within this larger context of migration throughout the British Empire and the African diaspora.

People of African descent have lived in the Maritimes since the early 1600s. These first black inhabitants were not necessarily enslaved. For example, around 1605, Mathieu Da Costa served as a paid translator between the Mi'kmaq and French. Other early Africans might have been servants, but they were not necessarily enslaved in the same way that black people throughout the Atlantic world would be during the 1700s. The first major incidence of slavery occurred in Île Royale (Cape Breton). Between 1713 and 1758, there were 266 slaves living there and the vast majority of them were black people. These slaves did not make up a large percentage of the colony's population.[5] They came from various regions including the American colonies, the West Indies, and Africa. Most Île Royale masters only owned a few slaves. These slaves worked in the domestic sphere, which included washing clothes, cooking, gardening, cutting firewood, nursing, moving hay, and shovelling snow. These slaves performed valuable tasks that allowed an owner's family to engage in other occupations. In Île Royale, there were small numbers of slaves per household, significant levels of interaction between owners and their slaves, and a mixed economic system where slaves acted as multi-occupational labourers (in this economy there was not a slave-produced staple such as tobacco, cotton, rice, or sugar). Slavery did not dominate the economic or political structure as it did in South Carolina or Jamaica. This society with slaves would be expanded in the ensuing decades as English-speaking settlers, including the Loyalists, migrated to the rest of the Maritimes.[6]

Slaveholders and their slaves became much more common in Nova Scotia after the founding of Halifax in 1749. This growing town became an integral part of the trading system between Europe, North America, the West Indies, and Africa. This economic exchange included timber, fish, molasses, sugar, salt, and slaves. In 1750, one Royal Navy officer brought 16 slaves to Nova Scotia (Document 68, p. 124). A Boston newspaper, one year later, advertised: "JUST arriv'd from Hallifax, and to be sold, Ten Hearty Strong Negro Men, mostly Tradesmen, such as Caulkers, Carpenters, Sailmakers, Ropemakers"

4 Harvey Amani Whitfield, "The African Diaspora in Atlantic Canada: History, Historians, and Historiography," *Acadiensis* 46 (Winter/Spring 2017): 213–32.

5 Kenneth Donovan estimates that slaves represented about three per cent of the population of Louisbourg, the capital of Île Royale; see Kenneth Donovan, "Slaves in Île Royale, 1713–1758," *French Colonial History* 5 (2004): 27.

6 Kenneth Donovan, "Slaves and Their Owners in Ile Royale, 1713–1760," *Acadiensis* 25 (Autumn 1995): 3–32; Kenneth Donovan, "A Nominal List of Slaves and Their Owners in Ile Royale, 1713–1760," *Nova Scotia Historical Review* 16 (1996): 151–62; Kenneth Donovan, "Slaves in Île Royale" 25–42; Kenneth Donovan, "Female Slaves as Sexual Victims in Ile Royale," *Acadiensis* 43 (Winter/Spring, 2014): 147–56.

(Document 1, p. 24). In 1752, a Halifax merchant offered several slaves for sale including a woman who he described as "A likely Negro Wench, of about thirty five years of Age, a Creole born [born in the New World], has been brought up in a Gentleman's family, and capable of doing all sorts of work belonging thereto ... every other Thing that can be expected from Such a Slave" (Document 2, p. 25).

Following the Acadian Expulsion (in which the British government forcibly removed the vast majority of Acadians from their land in the Maritimes and sent them to other colonies), Governor Charles Lawrence offered the expropriated land to English-speaking settlers from New England. The government further granted an additional 50 acres of land for each black person brought into the colony, thereby encouraging slavery in the region. As a result, some of the New England Planters brought slaves to Nova Scotia. Between 1759 and 1774, approximately 8,000 Planters settled in Nova Scotia. Historians do not know the exact number of Planter slaves who arrived in the Maritimes.[7] However, it is clear that these slaves and their owners were fully engaged in the larger British world and that Nova Scotia was hardly an outpost beyond the reaches of the Anglo-American world. In fact, it may be added that the New England Planters' use of slaves and their strengthening of slavery in the Maritime colonies underlined their similarity to other slaveholding areas throughout New England and New York. Like slaves in Île Royale, New England Planter slaves had close contact with their owners and worked in a mixed economy. Most slaves worked in a range of tasks such as planting crops, repairing fences, cooking, cleaning, and caring for children. The character of New England Planter slavery was perpetuated and expanded by Loyalist slave-owners and their slaves.[8]

Maritime slavery must be understood as part of several overlapping systems of black labour exploitation throughout the British world. The majority of Maritime slaves came from the American colonies including New England, the Middle Atlantic (New York, New Jersey, and Pennsylvania), the Chesapeake (Virginia, Maryland, Delaware), and the Deep South (South Carolina and Georgia). A few of these slaves originated in Africa and the

---

7 From her preliminary research, historian Karolyn Smardz Frost argues that there may have been as many as 200 Planter slaves (private conversation, 26 February 2015).

8 T. Stephen Henderson and Wendy G. Robicheau, eds., *Nova Scotia Planters in the Atlantic World, 1759–1830* (Fredericton: Acadiensis Press, 2012); Lucille H. Campey, *Planters, Paupers, and Pioneers: English Settlers in Atlantic Canada* (Toronto: Dundurn Press, 2010); George Rawlyk and Gordon T. Stewart, *A People Highly Favoured of God: The Nova Scotia Yankees and the American Revolution* (Toronto: Macmillan, 1972); Margaret Conrad, ed., *Making Adjustments: Change and Continuity in Planter Nova Scotia, 1759–1800* (Fredericton: Acadiensis Press, 1991); Margaret Conrad and Barry Moody, eds., *Planter Links: Community and Culture in Colonial Nova Scotia* (Fredericton: Acadiensis Press, 2001); Margaret Conrad, ed., *They Planted Well: New England Planters in Maritime Canada* (Fredericton: Acadiensis Press, 1988); Margaret Conrad, ed., *Intimate Relations: Family and Community in Planter Nova Scotia, 1759–1800* (Fredericton: Acadiensis Press, 1995).

Caribbean. Once these slaves arrived in the Maritimes, they used their traditions, family connections, and work experiences to navigate the living conditions of their new homes. In the Maritimes, they encountered a form of slavery that would have been familiar to those from New England and other northern colonies. At the outset of Loyalist settlement, most slaves lived briefly in Shelburne, but the poor land resulted in the town suffering from serious outmigration. As a result, most slaves relocated (if they were not taken back to the United States) to the Annapolis region of western Nova Scotia and Saint John, though slaves also settled throughout the Maritimes. Slaves usually lived with their owners and worked alongside them doing a variety of tasks. The intimate nature of slave/slaveholder relationships in the Maritimes could be a double-edged sword. In some cases, living with their owners might result in better treatment, but it could just as easily become an abusive relationship if slaves did not have the comfort of a large slave community or distance provided by living in slave cabins. Most Maritime slaves had to live in the same house as their owners and as a result they were on call 24 hours a day.

THE LEGAL STATUS OF SLAVERY

After the influx of American Loyalists and their slaves to the Maritimes, slavery was widespread and racism became increasingly entrenched. It is a mistake, however, to see the region as monolithically dedicated to both slavery and racism. Though slavery remained strong, it was highly contested by anti-slavery legislators, judges, lawyers, and religious groups. The number of slaves increased after the Loyalist influx, but slavery remained legally insecure and somewhat unstable, because though it was recognized under common law as a form of private property, this had no statutory basis (such as a slave code) in Nova Scotia or New Brunswick. In Prince Edward Island, an act that dealt with slave baptism gave statute recognition to slavery (Document 69, p. 125). The tenuousness of slavery is highlighted by the numerous attempts by owners to gain statute protection for their property (in 1787, 1789, 1801, and 1808 in Nova Scotia, and in 1801 in New Brunswick). They were defeated each time.[9] Yet Maritime slavery seems to

9 *Journal and Proceedings of the House of Assembly* [hereafter *JHOA*], (Halifax: King's Printer 1787), 17 and 22, Nova Scotia Archives [hereafter NSA], Halifax, Nova Scotia; An Act for the Regulation and Relief of the Free Negroes Within the Province of Nova Scotia, In Council, 2 April 1789, RG 5, Series U, Un-passed Bills, 1762–1792, NSA; *JHOA*, 1801, 72, NSA; A Bill relating to Negroes, 6 February 1801, Legislative Assembly Records, RS 24, S 14-B 9, Provincial Archives of New Brunswick [hereafter PANB], Fredericton, New Brunswick; An Act for regulating Negro Servants within and throughout this Province, 1808, RG 5, Series U, Un-passed Bills, NSA.

have lasted into the early 1820s, and owners constantly fought in the courts and legislatures to protect their alleged right to own slaves.

Between 1783 and 1785, a complex mix of American slaves, from East Florida to northern Massachusetts, settled in the Maritimes. Due to the limitations of evidence, historians cannot give an exact number of Loyalist slaves in the Maritimes. Estimates range from about 1,500 to 2,000. The reason we cannot give an accurate number is due to the ambiguities in the documentation. It is not always explicit if an individual was actually enslaved.[10] **Chattel** slaves were often called "servants," a practice that makes it difficult to distinguish between free black servants and those who remained enslaved after arriving in the Maritimes. As the historian Robin Winks noted, there "is no way to know how many of the several thousand Negroes in the Maritime provinces were slaves and how many were free."[11] He believed that the reason for the indiscriminate usage of "slave" and "servant" reflected an increasing concern about the morality of slavery. He suggests that though "most 'servants' were slaves," others were either free black children or **indentured** adults.[12] Slave-owners and slaves struggled to redefine what slavery meant by partially relying on past experiences while confronting the new realities of settlement, climate, soil, and economy. Slaves had to reconstitute families and friendships, while learning new work patterns and how to grow new crops with different seasons. Certainly, this experience differed by slave. Those from New York or New England probably experienced the greatest continuity between their old and new homes, while those from South Carolina or Maryland faced more rigorous adjustments. The first years after the Loyalist influx to the Maritimes were devoted to defining a system of slavery that was complicated by the large population of free Black Loyalists, the lack of clarity regarding slavery's legal status, and the willingness of Loyalist slaves to abscond and challenge the emerging social order, so that they could win freedom, gain autonomy, and reunite or protect their families from predatory owners.[13]

Chattel: Slaves were considered the personal property of their owners, and could be bought and sold at the whim of the owner.

indentured: An indentured servant is bound to a master for a set term, usually less than seven years.

In the Maritimes after the American Revolution, the labels of "free," "servant," or "slave" could quickly change if a person ran away or was re-enslaved. This is probably the most significant issue to understand about black life in the late eighteenth and early nineteenth century. A black person might arrive in New Brunswick as a slave only to escape from her owner before being recaptured and sold to the West Indies. Another individual could begin his sojourn in Nova Scotia as a free person, be subjected to indentured servitude,

10 Harvey Amani Whitfield, *North to Bondage: Loyalist Slavery in the Maritimes* (Vancouver: U of British Columbia P, 2016), 10–12, 119–20.

11 Winks, *Blacks*, 45.

12 Winks, *Blacks*, 45–46.

13 For a full listing of works related to the Black Loyalists, see *North to Bondage*, 132–34.

followed by re-enslavement, eventually escape, and finally enjoy freedom in Sierra Leone. The case of Lydia Jackson is instructive. Originally, she settled at Manchester (Guysborough Township) with other free blacks. As a result of poverty and the desertion of her husband, Jackson indentured herself to a Loyalist for what she thought would be a short time. It turned out that this person had tricked Jackson into signing an indenture that essentially made her a servant for life. This man then sold Jackson as a slave to a Dr. Bulman (or Bolman). As the doctor's slave, Jackson suffered from brutal mistreatment. Bulman regularly beat "her with the tongs, sticks, pieces of rope &c. about the head and face."[14] John Clarkson, a Royal Navy officer and organizer of the Black Loyalist exodus to Sierra Leone in 1792, noted that eventually Jackson escaped to Halifax. Jackson's owner planned on "selling her to some planter in the West Indies to work as a slave."[15] Lydia Jackson's story must be considered in the context of Clarkson's following comment: "I do not know what induced me to mention the above case as I have many others of a similar nature; for example, Scott's case, Mr. Lee, Senr. case, Smith's child, Motley Roads child, Mr. Farish's negro servant, &c" (Document 46, p. 83).

In the case of re-enslavement, historians can only speculate about how many black people were kidnapped and sold to the West Indies whose stories never made it before a court.[16] The kidnapping of black people in Nova Scotia became widespread enough that legislators attempted in 1789 to pass "An Act for the Regulation and Relief of the Free Negroes within the Province of Nova Scotia." Although the bill failed, it noted that "attempts have been made to carry some of them out of the Province, by force and Strategem for the scandalous purpose of making property of them in the West Indies contrary to their will and consent" (Document 72, p. 129).[17] Based on information from a local observer (possibly his brother John), the anti-slavery advocate Thomas Clarkson argued that whites reduced "again to slavery those negroes who had so honourably obtained their freedom. They hired them as servants, and, at the end of the stipulated time, refused payment of their wages, insisting that they were slaves: in some instances they destroyed their tickets of freedom, and then enslaved the [N]egroes for want of them; in several instances, the unfortunate Africans were taken onboard vessels, carried to the West Indies, and there sold for the benefit of their plunderers" (Document 47, p. 84).

---

14 C.B. Fergusson, ed., *Clarkson's Mission to America, 1791–1792* (Halifax: Public Archives of Nova Scotia, 1971), 90.

15 *Ibid.*

16 *Ibid.*

17 An Act for the Regulation and Relief of the Free Negroes Within the Province of Nova Scotia, In Council, 2 April 1789, RG 5, Series U, Box 1, 1762–1792, NSA.

BLACK SERVANTS AND BLACK SLAVES

The line between black servants and black slaves was extremely fluid and could easily be transgressed and manipulated. Even those blacks who were indentured servants were often treated as slaves and consistently faced the fear of being sold to the West Indies or elsewhere. To what extent did white Loyalists distinguish between an indentured black servant and a black slave? More importantly, did indentured black servants and slaves see each other as having different statuses? Black servants and black slaves ran away together sometimes from the same master. For example, South Carolina Loyalist Nathaniel Bullern, complained about the loss of, "TWO NEGRO—the Property of Mr. Nath. Bullern, the One an indented Servant, the Other a Slave" (Document 13, p. 41). These two people were, servant and slave, both part of a world of "unfreedom."[18] In running away together, they saw their status as similar if not the same. Jupiter and Clarinda had both arrived in Nova Scotia as slaves, but shortly after arrival Bullern had freed one of them.[19] Several court cases in Shelburne in the 1780s and 1790s show how easily black people could fall victim to re-enslavement, but also the ways in which they could go to court, defeat attempts at re-enslavement, and achieve freedom. The first years after the Loyalist influx were, at best, confusing and complicated in terms of the changing status of free black, black servant, and black slave. Runaway advertisements included black indentured servants and black servants, but were these people essentially enslaved? Obviously, it would depend on their masters, but black servants operated in a world where they could easily be sold as slaves to the United States or the West Indies. Were their lives any different than their enslaved brethren? Again, the answer varied by individual.

THE NATURE OF MARITIME SLAVERY

There are three aspects of slavery that readers must understand. First, slave-holding reached into most socio-economic classes of white society, with artisans, small business owners, and small farmers possessing one or two slaves. For example, Thomas Bean and John DeMill were both registered

18 Jared Ross Hardesty, *Unfreedom: Slavery and Dependence in Eighteenth-Century Boston* (New York: New York UP, 2016).

19 Book of Negroes, Sir Guy Carleton Papers, National Archives (UK), microfilm copy at NSA. Clarinda (age 19) and Jupiter (age 33) are listed one after the other. Clarinda seems to have been the property of Henry Boyd before becoming the property of Dr. Bullern. The way Bullern wrote his runaway advertisement makes it somewhat unclear exactly which one was enslaved.

as carpenters in Saint John. DeMill owned one male slave in his twenties, while Bean possessed a young teenager named Keziah (or Kezzia).[20]

Second, the close proximity of Maritime slaves and their owners resulted in the same type of "family" bondage that typified slavery in New England and most parts of the Middle Colonies. Family slavery is the best way to understand the relationships between the vast majority of Maritime slaves and slaveholders. Historians have long recognized the close interactions of slave-owners and slaves in New England and other northern states. African American slaves worked next to their owners, ate with them, and slept in the same houses. This proximity made slaves part of the household and family they served.[21] In the Maritimes, both slaves and slaveholders were explicitly conscious of the notion of belonging to a family. For instance, a "sickly" slave named Dinah, on her way from New York to Nova Scotia commented that she had "always been in the family" of her owner.[22] Dinah's words reflected an expectation that her master should provide for her medical care after years of service. The notion of belonging to a family does not mean that slavery in New England or the Maritime colonies should be understood as benevolent or mild. Maritime slaveholders exploited black labour and regularly broke apart black families no matter how long slaves had been members (though clearly inferior ones) of their owner's family. As the historian William Piersen has argued, "the closeness of master and bondsmen often created ties of deep and abiding affection, the duty of one to rule and of the other to obey led to unavoidable frustrations for both, frustrations which constantly chafed the ideal of paternalistic harmony."[23] As the documents demonstrate, the intimate interactions between Maritime slaves and slave-owners were contradictory and ran the gamut from expressions and acts of true affection and kindness to violent and sadistic outbursts.

Third and most importantly, we must understand that slaves were far from powerless. They regularly negotiated aspects of their bondage or broke the bonds of slavery through flight (see Part I). This is not to deny the blatant and brutal exploitation of enslaved people, but rather to understand that they could partially influence their own circumstances despite being slaves.

Enslaved people sometimes exerted their agency through absconding. This was often done to keep their families from being separated. Local records are full of instances of children removed from their parents' care (see Document 56, p. 103). As such, it is not surprising that some slave families decided to flee rather than see themselves torn apart. At times, running away

---

20 Wright, *Loyalists*, 259 and 276; Book of Negroes.

21 Piersen, *Black Yankees*, 25–36.

22 Book of Negroes.

23 Piersen, *Black Yankees*, 36.

could be an attempt to reunite families, while some slave families escaped to leave a violent or otherwise difficult situation. Other reasons for leaving included mistreatment or forced sexual relations between a master and an slave. These families escaped to retain some sense of control over their family lives. They ran away as families because of the importance of these relationships. They would have had a better opportunity to escape and hide as individuals, yet they preferred to remain together as families even if this lessened their chance of gaining permanent freedom. In 1785, "A Man, his Wife, and two Children, *James, Bet, Frank, and Judy*" escaped from their owner Samuel Andrews (Document 14, p. 42), but Andrews later recaptured them. This slave family probably absconded because of their treatment at Andrews's hands or because he planned to sell them.

THE GRADUAL ENDING OF SLAVERY

One of the more striking things about Maritime slavery is that the region did not adopt any legislation ending slavery. Indeed, every New England state along with Pennsylvania, New York and New Jersey had adopted immediate or gradual emancipation by 1804, while the Maritimes did not enact similar legislation with the exception of Prince Edward Island's 1825 repeal of the 1781 Slave Baptism Act (Documents 69 and 74, pp. 125 and 132). In the other parts of British North America, Upper and Lower Canada, slavery was slowly abolished judicially and legislatively. In the late 1790s, Chief Justice James Monk issued a series of decisions that made, "slavery virtually untenable in Lower Canada."[24] In Upper Canada, the legislature passed "An Act to Prevent the further introduction of SLAVES," which banned importation of slaves and freed the children of slaves once they reached the age of 25. Nova Scotia and New Brunswick did not adopt gradual emancipation because neither colony had statute law, such as a slave code, protecting slavery and therefore most assemblymen deemed it unnecessary.

Although the influx of Loyalist slave-owners and their slaves greatly expanded and strengthened slavery, it left the institution vulnerable. The categories of slave, servant, and free black became contingent and unstable. Nova Scotia and New Brunswick did not have statute law related to slavery, leaving a space for black and white people to negotiate and understand the perimeters of slavery. Slaveholders regularly went to court to retrieve runaway slaves or to re-enslave free blacks, while slaves went to court to challenge owners' rights to hold them in bondage. From the moment they stepped onto the shores of the Maritimes, slaves took an active role in

24 Winks, *Blacks*, 102.

obtaining their own freedom by running away and finding sympathetic whites willing to support their claims in court. Until the mid-1790s, Nova Scotian judges sometimes returned escaped slaves to their supposed owners (see Document 59, p. 107). Subsequently, Chief Justices Thomas Strange and S.S. Blowers made it nearly impossible for owners to prove they held legal title to their slaves. In contrast, the conservative legal and political culture of New Brunswick ensured that judges upheld slavery or at least left it alone (see Documents 62 and 67, pp. 114 and 119). Historian David Bell suggests that its judges were protesting the intellectual tides of the early nineteenth century as illustrated by Nova Scotia's judicial elimination of slavery, the growing agitation against the slave trade, and the adoption of gradual or immediate emancipation in most northern states. They believed that a class of gentlemen connected to the Crown should rule society. From this perspective, ending slavery signalled not progressive social policy, but rather another step toward a state of anarchy where people did not accept their God-given places in society. "In a society like that of New Brunswick," Bell notes, "in which the position of the great was precarious, it may have been with considerable gratification that three of the judges ensured, as a matter of law, that the province's Negroes would continue to be very low indeed."[25] Slavery in New Brunswick did not end until the early 1820s because the judiciary did not follow the footsteps of Strange and Blowers in Nova Scotia.

Eventually, slavery ended in the Maritimes because slaves pushed back against their owners and won their freedom with the help of local anti-slavery whites. They were supported in this endeavour by an increasingly broad swath of the white Maritime population during the early nineteenth century. The majority of politicians and everyday people were not willing to give statute recognition to slavery. Moreover, sympathetic whites harboured runaways and willingly challenged slaveholders in court. The supporters of slavery became an ever smaller and isolated group. By the early 1800s, well-known slave-owners such as Stair Agnew, Joseph Clarke, James DeLancey, Jesse Gray, and Caleb Jones simply did not represent the majority of opinion in the region. Others inclined to own slaves could leave the Maritimes for the West Indies or the United States. In many ways, the ending of slavery can be seen as a positive example of black–white cooperation where humanitarian impulses played an important role in destroying slavery. But, the other reason slavery ended is economic.

The use of free black labour, which began in the 1780s and expanded during the next 25 years, made chattel bondage unnecessary. The eventual

---

25 Bell, "Judges of Loyalist New Brunswick," 31. On Early Saint John, see D.G. Bell, *Early Loyalist Saint John: The Origin of New Brunswick Politics, 1783–1786* (Fredericton: New Ireland P, 1983); also see David Bell, *Loyalist Rebellion in New Brunswick: A Defining Conflict for Canada's Political Culture* (Halifax: Formac, 2013).

switch to cheap black labour should not be seen as inevitable or easy. For slaveholders, the loss of a capital asset that could be sold out of the region represented a serious financial hit. If slavery had ended suddenly, the loss of human property would have been catastrophic for a slaveholder's financial standing. Yet, as we know, slavery did not end immediately, but rather very gradually and slowly, which gave slave-owners plenty of time to devise other methods to still benefit from their slaves. First, they sold slaves out of the region to the West Indies or the United States, which simply continued a well-trodden path embraced by slaveholders for decades. Second, in substituting forms of indentured servitude for chattel slavery, former owners could still benefit from their black servants during some of their best and most productive years. Slave-owners usually freed slaves when they reached their twenties and in some cases not until they were 30.[26] Slaveholders also hired out slaves to other residents, which gave the owners another revenue stream.[27] They continued to exploit black people even after they were offered conditional freedom (Document 50, p. 89). From the perspective of slaveholders, free black labour was not necessarily as good as slave labour which they could sell, but eventually it did serve as a decent substitute for those who had previously owned slaves. Once slavery had disappeared from the region, black labour could be further exploited through a system of gross inequities and racial discrimination without the stain of slavery on the region. Free blacks and black indentured servants did similar forms of labour—multi-occupational work ranging from farm labour to carpentry—to that which slaves had done. In the final analysis, slavery gradually ended in the Maritimes because of black agency, growing numbers of anti-slavery whites, and sympathetic judges.

MARITIME BLACK CULTURE

The Maritimes were home to a broad range of black cultures. North American slaves employed their traditions and beliefs to fashion autonomous spaces of material, oral, and expressive community. Conscious of their African heritage, Maritime slaves forged an authentic slave culture within the parameters of their white environment. In New Brunswick, one slave-owner noted that his runaway, "attempts to play the VIOLIN" (Document 23, p. 51). Violins held an important place in American slave culture and were prevalent in parts of West Africa. According to the historian Sterling

26 Isaac Bonnell, 1806, Annapolis County, RG 48, Probate Records, NSA; Jacob Troop, 1805, Annapolis County, RG 48, Probate Records, NSA; George Cornwall, 1799, Annapolis County, RG 48, Probate Records, NSA.

27 T.W. Smith, "The Slave in Canada," *Collections of the Nova Scotia Historical Society*, 10 (1899): 116.

"A black wood cutter at Shelburne, Nova Scotia" by Captain William Booth. This is one of the first known depictions of an African Nova Scotian.

Stuckey, the violin became "the most important instrument of slave musicians and important among northern slaves as well."[28] Most Loyalist slaves were either from New England or the Middle Colonies, and they brought their experiences and traditions with them to the Maritimes. Throughout these regions, cultural activities such as Negro Election Day and the Pinkster Festival gained popularity. These events were multiracial, black and white people participated, and local newspapers commented on each event. On Negro Election Day, slaves elected an individual among them to a ceremonial office, though the unofficial nature of the post by no means implies this person could not exercise real influence among the black population. On the other hand, Pinkster (originally a Dutch religious holiday that could be a day of rest or used for religious ceremonies like baptism) encompassed several days of traditional African dancing, sporting events, and the crowning

28 Sterling Stuckey, *Slave Culture: Nationalist Theory and the Foundations of Black America* (New York: Oxford UP, 1987), 21.

of a king.[29] Aspects of these activities accompanied northern slaves to the Maritimes and were termed "Negro Frolicks" in Shelburne, which hardly captures the cultural significance of these celebrations. These "Frolicks" were banned in 1785 for two possible reasons. First, the festivals were loud and gave rise to what officials perceived as rowdy behaviour. Second, slave-owners realized that these celebrations could have been spaces for increased solidarity among slaves and free blacks or sites where slaves made elaborate runaway plans. Whatever the case, these dances embodied deeply held religious and spiritual values and were an expression of African aesthetics, which was also reinforced by the presence of free blacks.

There are two other aspects of slave culture that deserve attention: slave clothing and baptism. In an important article, Shane White and Graham White demonstrated how slaves used clothing to appropriate "items of elite apparel," display "an almost bewildering variety in slave apparel," and carve out a "surprising degree of social and cultural space."[30] Runaway advertisements in the Maritimes show that slaves carved out their own cultural space by appropriating fancier clothing than usually afforded to slaves (Documents 24, 26, 33, pp. 52, 54, and 62). These clothes could have held status meanings not only for the wider society, but also within the black community. Apparel represented the property individual slaves had been able to accumulate. Slaves' clothing offered them control over their own bodies by fashioning for public view the image they wanted others to see. Maritime slaves also lived in a community with a substantial free black population. Perhaps, through the use of certain clothing, slaves were attempting to project how they thought free blacks should appear. The opportunity to gain some modicum of control over their bodies and appearance made the use of clothing a significant part of black culture and slave self-expression.

Slaves were baptized throughout the Maritimes. The records of these baptisms are scattered throughout township and church records. For instance, in 1793, "Jane, Dinah, Samuel, Negro children property of B. Belcher Esq.," were baptized.[31] Masters and slaves probably had varied and complicated

29 James Oliver Horton and Lois E. Horton, *In Hope of Liberty: Culture, Community and Protest Among Northern Free Blacks, 1700–1860* (New York: Oxford UP, 1997), 22–24 and 30–33; for excellent work on these festivals, see Piersen, *Black Yankees*, 117–40; Shane White, "'It Was a Proud Day': African Americans, Festivals, and Parades in the North, 1741–1834," *Journal of American History* 81 (1994): 13–50; Joseph P. Reidy, "Negro Election Day and Black Community Life in New England, 1750–1860," *Marxist Perspectives* 1 (1978): 102–17; on Christianity and other cultural beliefs and activities, see Graham Russell Hodges, *Root & Branch: African Americans in New York & East Jersey, 1613–1863* (Chapel Hill: U of North Carolina P, 1999), 115–28.

30 Shane White and Graham White, "Slave Clothing and African-American Culture in the Eighteenth and Nineteenth Centuries," *Past and Present* 148 (1995): 150, 155.

31 Cornwallis Township Book, June 1793, p. 8, MG 4, Vol. 18–18A, NSA; also see St. Paul's Anglican Church Baptismal Records, Amelia Byers, John Byers, Edward Byers, William Byers, 1795, Public Archives and Records Office, Prince Edward Island, Charlottetown, Prince Edward Island [hereafter PAROPEI].

understandings of baptism's meaning. Slaveholders probably baptized their slaves to follow the Great Commission of making disciples throughout the world (Matthew 28:18–20).[32] Like their American cousins, Maritime slaveholders could certainly have used parts of the New Testament to justify slaveholding and their exploitation of black labour (Ephesians 6:5–7).[33] According to historian Albert Raboteau, slaves might have believed that, "baptism would raise their status and lead eventually to freedom for their children, if not themselves."[34] Some slaves from the southern states might have interpreted baptism differently than their counterparts from New England. At the same time, those slaves from Africa or with parents from Africa might have seen baptism in light of their own traditions. The meaning of baptism also could have been a way to negotiate for greater rights *within* the system of slavery. Perhaps slaves also saw baptism as a path to freedom or possibly better treatment from their owners. For some African societies, water and rivers held an important place in individuals' religious understanding and could have purifying or regenerative purposes. These are not the only aspects of slave culture, but the lack of documentation on the Maritimes makes it difficult for historians to say more about this topic. Hopefully, future scholars will find more documentation to offer a fuller and more satisfying picture of slave culture.

MONEY AND SLAVES

Generally speaking, readers should consider the following basic conversion chart when reading through the documents:

12 pennies = 1 shilling
20 shillings = 1 pound
21 shillings = 1 guinea

The pricing of slaves in the Maritimes is difficult to assess. There are not nearly enough documents recording slave prices to offer anything

32 Matthew 28:18–20. Then Jesus came to them and said, "All authority in heaven and on earth has been given to me. Therefore go and make disciples of all nations, baptizing them in the name of the Father and of the Son and of the Holy Spirit, and teaching them to obey everything I have commanded you. And surely I am with you always, to the very end of the age."

33 Ephesians 6:5-7. Slaves, obey your earthly masters with respect and fear, and with sincerity of heart, just as you would obey Christ. Obey them not only to win their favor when their eye is on you, but as slaves of Christ, doing the will of God from your heart. Serve wholeheartedly, as if you were serving the Lord, not people.

34 Albert J. Raboteau, *Canaan Land: A Religious History of African Americans* (Oxford: Oxford UP, 1999), 16.

approaching an overall estimate of the precise value of slaves. Also, why owners assigned slaves certain prices or offered varying rewards for runaway slaves remains unclear. Most documents simply mention the value of a slave and sometimes sex and age, but rarely anything about skill level. It is not always clear whether the currency listed is in sterling, Halifax currency, or another legal tender. According to economic historian Julian Gwyn, "the par value between Halifax currency and sterling was H£1.11 [Halifax pounds] to £1.00."[35] He adds that, during the late 1780s, a common labourer's daily wage in the Annapolis Valley was 75 cents.[36] Despite Gwyn's helpful context, any assessment of slave prices is rather impressionistic, but it does provide insight into how slave-owners valued their slaves. In various documents ranging from estate inventories to bills of sales to rewards for runaways, the price of slaves varied tremendously. For example, in May 1783, John Wilson offered "Two Guineas" reward for his young escaped male slave.[37] Slightly over one year later, in July 1784, Frederick William Hecht offered "Five Guineas" reward for Hector, who was a cooper.[38] Most adults were valued at between £25 and £60, with the majority worth around £30 or £40. The prices of slave children ranged from £5 (in 1786) to at least £42 (in 1804).[39] In 1779, before the Loyalist influx, one 12-year-old male slave named Abram commanded the price of £50.[40] In an estate inventory from 1796, a Halifax slave-owner listed his "black girl" named Sary as worth £30.[41] In 1804 in Annapolis County, the estate of Robert Dickson sold eight-year-old Percilla for £17 to William Robertson.[42] Four years later, Sarah Allen sold 14-year-old Bacchus to Titus Knapp for £30.[43] The price of adult slaves also varied drastically over time and it is not exactly clear why one slave was worth more than another. In 1786, Richard Betts's slave Jane was valued at £35, while 10 years later Bethaser Creamer's slave Mary was valued at £60. Creamer also listed his adult male slave Benjamin as worth £60.[44] In 1802, Dr. Bond purchased Kate for £40.[45] These sums must be set within the contextual reality that

---

35 Julian Gwyn, *Excessive Expectations: Maritime Commerce & the Economic Development of Nova Scotia* (Montreal-Kingston: McGill-Queen's UP, 1998), 32; also see John J. McCusker, *Money and Exchange in Europe and America, 1600–1775: A Handbook* (Chapel Hill: U of North Carolina P, 1978).

36 Gwyn, *Excessive Expectations*, 23.

37 *Nova Scotia Gazette and Weekly Chronicle*, 20 May 1783.

38 *Saint John Gazette*, 15 July 1784.

39 Smith, "Slave," 66–67; Joseph Totten, 1788, Annapolis County, RG 48, Probate Records, NSA.

40 Slavery in Colchester, Sale of Slave, 29 September 1779, F 142, Slavery, William Cochrane Milner Fonds, S 13, F135–F154, New Brunswick Museum [hereafter NBM].

41 Smith, "Slave," 94.

42 Sale of a Slave, MG 100, vol. 103, #F3a, NSA.

43 Smith, "Slave," 67.

44 Smith, "Slave," 94.

45 Smith, "Slave," 64.

the Maritimes experienced a postwar depression from 1784 to at least 1792. A study of individual slave prices within a household is more revealing.[46]

The 1786 inventory of Richard Betts listed four slaves and their values. According to the document, Toney, Prince (or Primus), and Jane were listed as worth £35, while Harry commanded the price of £40. It is not clear why Harry was worth more money. Perhaps he was a skilled slave, or the other slaves were older or more troublesome from the owner's perspective. We cannot know. The total value of Betts's inventory was about £1053, while the combined value of the slaves was £145.[47] Thus, slaves accounted for 13.77 per cent of the total wealth of his estate. The Annapolis county resident Joseph Totten's 1788 inventory listed five slaves, including two adults and three children. Totten recorded the three children as being worth a total of £15, or £5 for each individual child. His "Negro Wench" was valued at £60, while a "Negro Boy" cost about £50. Totten noted that the currency he used was "New York Money" to the total of £125, which he converted to about £78. Taken together, they were worth more than half a lot of land he owned in the town of Annapolis, which he valued at £150.[48] The precise age of Totten's adult slaves or the skills they possessed are unknown.[49] Betts and Totten made their wills during an economic downturn and this probably affected the appraisal of their slaves. Both men lived relatively nearby one another with Betts at Granville and Totten at Annapolis Royal. The low value that Totten placed on his child slaves might be indicative of a general attitude among local slaveholders that they cost their owners money and might not become productive for several years.

Some estate inventories reveal that, except for actual real estate, slaves were usually worth more than other property ranging from furniture to livestock. For example, Totten's horse, wagon, three cows, case of pistols, and one silver watch were worth a total of £46, much less than his slaves, whose combined value was about £78. In 1801, a Yarmouth slaveholder purchased

---

46 Sources consulted for this section include, Smith, "Slave," 62–67 and 94; *Douglass v. MacNeill*, 1791, Halifax, vol. 62, no. 62, RG 39 C, NSA; *King v. Jesse Gray*, 9 November 1786, Shelburne, vol. 27, #27.2, RG 60, NSA; Slavery in Colchester, Sale of Slave, 29 September 1779, F 142 NBM; Slavery, William Cochrane Milner Fonds, S 13, F135–F154, NBM; Richard Betts, 1786 Annapolis County, RG 48, Probate Records, NSA; Joseph Totten, 1788, Annapolis County RG 48, Probate Records, NSA; J.R. Campbell, *A History of the County of Yarmouth, Nova Scotia* (Saint John: J & A McMillan, 1876), 145; *Daily Sun* (Saint John), 29 August 1890; *Times* (Moncton), 27 October 1880; Sale of a Slave, MG 100, vol. 103, #F3a, NSA; Sale of a Slave, William Cochrane Milner Fonds, F 47A, Slavery, NBM; Richard Wilson slave sale, 19 August 1793, NSA; Thomas Chandler slave sale, 27 January 1792, NSA.

47 Richard Betts, 1786 Annapolis County, RG 48, Probate Records, NSA.

48 McCusker, *Money and Exchange*, 165. Also see John J. McCusker, *How Much Is That in Real Money: A Historical Price Index for Use as a Deflator of Money Values in the Economy of the United States* (Worcester: American Antiquarian Society, 1992).

49 Joseph Totten, 1788, Annapolis County, RG 48, Probate Records, NSA.

a seven-year-old slave named Jack for £39.[50] In comparison, Stephen Reed's 1801 inventory lists four oxen and one heifer as worth £35.[51] In the late 1780s in Shelburne, Jesse Gray sold Mary Postell in the same town for 100 bushels of potatoes, and Benjamin Douglas purchased a 22-year-old female for £50 (Halifax currency) in another region of Nova Scotia. The prices of Loyalist slaves varied over time and place.[52]

A NOTE ON THE DOCUMENTS

Before readers delve into the documents, it is essential to understand the humanity of these enslaved people. The system of slavery was inhumane, exploitative and exceedingly brutal. It turned human beings into financial commodities who were treated as undeserving of the most basic form of human dignity. Historians must never underestimate the fear and violence that formed the basis of slavery. Yet it is a mistake to assume that enslaved people had no agency or ability to determine certain aspects of their lives. To put it bluntly, slaves had cards that they could play against their owners. They rarely had good cards to play, but that did not mean they could never win a hand. Maritime slaves had agency in their dealings with individual owners. They could run away, demand better treatment, work listlessly until given what they wanted, and negotiate their own freedom. It is easy to imagine slaves as having the exact same experience and being passive victims during slavery and the emancipation movement. These documents tell a very different story. If readers study the following documents with attention, the variety of experiences and actions of slaves, slaveholders, and others will become abundantly clear. The complexity of the political and cultural context of Maritime slavery must be understood on three intertwined levels: the regional, national/continental, imperial/global. Most Maritime slaves migrated from the Caribbean, the American colonies, and Africa. Their experiences in these various contexts informed how they dealt with slavery in the Maritimes. This book will give readers the opportunity to explore the lived experience of black slaves in pre-Confederation Canada.

I acquired the documents for this sourcebook over a 10-year period during which I wrote *North to Bondage: Loyalist Slavery in the Maritimes* (2016). After writing *Blacks on the Border: The Black Refugees in British North America, 1815–1860* (2006), I wanted to explore the history of slavery in the

50 J.R. Campbell, *A History of the County of Yarmouth, Nova Scotia* (Saint John: J. & A. McMillan, 1876), 145.

51 Stephen Reed, 1801, Cumberland County, RG 48, Probate Records, NSA.

52 *Douglass v. MacNeill*, 1791, Halifax, vol. 62, no. 62, RG 39 C, NSA; *King v. Jesse Gray*, 9 November 1786, Shelburne, vol. 27, #27.2, RG 60, NSA.

Maritimes. I knew there were slaves in Nova Scotia, New Brunswick, and Prince Edward Island because of the Loyalists. But I knew little about them. Who were these people? Where were they from? What types of work did they do in the Maritimes? What experiences and traditions did they bring to the Maritimes? Why had so much attention been lavished on the free Black Loyalists at the expense of these slaves? These questions resulted in my combing through a combination of archives in Britain, Canada, and the United States. More specifically, the majority of my documents were found at libraries and archives in New Brunswick, Nova Scotia, and Prince Edward Island. The Nova Scotia Archives, Provincial Archives of New Brunswick, the Loyalist Collection at University of New Brunswick, and the Prince Edward Island Archives were indispensable sources for finding court cases, government documents, runaway slave advertisements, and probate records about slavery.

I have attempted to transcribe the documents as carefully as possible. In some instances, I have modernized certain spellings or edited certain documents to make them more readable, but in the majority of cases I attempted to transcribe the documents as they were written. I hope that readers will find the editorial comments and transcription helpful.

CHRONOLOGY

c. 1605	Mathieu Da Costa is probably the first person of African descent to live in Nova Scotia. He served as a translator for the French.
1713–1815	Several hundred slaves lived in Île Royale (Cape Breton). The majority of them were black.
1749	Halifax founded.
1751	Halifax slaves offered for sale in Boston (Document 1, p. 24).
1755–64	Acadian Expulsion.
1760–74	New England Planters settle in Nova Scotia along with their slaves.
1781	Prince Edward Island Slave Baptism Act (Document 69, p. 125).
1783	Arrival of at least 30,000 Loyalists in Nova Scotia; several thousand free Black Loyalists and Loyalist slaves.
1785	Petition of Zimri Armstrong about re-enslavement (Document 43, p. 76).
1788	James MacGregor published *A Letter to a Clergyman Urging him to set free a Black Girl he held in SLAVERY* (Document 44, p. 78).
1789	An Act for the Regulation & Relief of the free Negroes within the Province of Nova Scotia (unpassed) (Document 72, p. 129).
1790	Petition of Thomas Peters to the British Government decrying conditions facing slaves and free blacks in the Maritimes (Document 45, p. 79).
1791	Mary Postell court case—a black woman and her children re-enslaved (Document 59, p. 107).
1796–1800	550 Jamaican Maroons in Halifax.
1800	Supreme Court "Nancy" case—New Brunswick Court divided and Nancy returned to slavery (Document 62, p. 114).

1801 A Bill Relating to Negroes, New Brunswick (unpassed) (Document 73, p. 131).

1802 Prince Edward Island Supreme Court returned slave to his owner (Document 65, p. 117).

1803–04 James DeLancey Court Case—Nova Scotian slave-owner did not obtain his runaway slave (Document 61, p. 112).

1806 New Brunswick Supreme Court case—a victory for slave-owners (Document 67, p. 119).

1807 Digby slave-owners' petition, Nova Scotia (Document 53, p. 93).

1807 Britain and United States Outlaw Atlantic Slave Trade

1813–16 Around 3,200 black refugees settled in the Maritimes during and after the War of 1812.[1]

1825 Prince Edward Island repealed Slave Baptism Act (Document 74, p. 132).

1833 Slavery Abolition Act (Britain)

1834 Petition of Isaac Willoughby, former slave (Document 54, p. 97).

1 Harvey Amani Whitfield, "The African Diaspora in Atlantic Canada: History, Historians, and Historiography," *Acadiensis* 46 (Winter/Spring 2017): 213.

QUESTIONS TO CONSIDER

1. Why are Canadians more familiar with the Black Loyalists and the Underground Railroad than with the origins and development of slavery in Canada?
2. Why are runaway slave advertisements one of the most important sources for the study of slavery? What do they tell us about slaves and slave-owners?
3. What were the connections between slavery in the Maritime colonies and the Caribbean?
4. What role did the Loyalists play in the expansion of slavery in the Maritimes?
5. Why is the case of Lydia Jackson (Document 46, p. 81) so important to understanding the ways in which free black people were re-enslaved?
6. What does the Digby slaveholder petition (Document 53, p. 93) say about the slaveholders' wider relationship to the United States and the British Empire? What can the reader learn about the actual slaves from this petition?
7. How did Maritime owners justify slavery and racism (Documents 51, 52, pp. 91 and 92)?
8. How did anti-slavery individuals argue against slavery (Documents 44, 63, pp. 78 and 115)?
9. How did free blacks and black slaves describe their experiences in bondage (Documents 43, 54, 59, pp. 76, 97, and 107)?
10. What does the PEI slavery statute and its repeal say about the role of religion in slavery (Documents 69, 74, pp. 125 and 132)?
11. Why is the example of Diana Bastian's resistance to George More so significant in the context of female slavery (Document 79, p. 140)?
12. What do wills tell historians about the relationship between slave-holders and their slaves?

PART I

Runaway Slave Advertisements and Slave for Sale Notices

Slaves were actual living and breathing people, and historians must try to recover as much as possible about their lives—who they were, where they lived, what work they did, who they married, their physical appearance, their personality traits, and whether they secured freedom. The sources will not allow us to answer all of these important questions about an individual slave's life. But runaway notices and for sale advertisements illuminate the lives of slaves in ways that historians might not be able to document otherwise.[1] In running away, slaves asserted their autonomy, rejected the violence that was inherent in the system of slavery, reunited and protected families, and cast doubt on the place of slavery in the Maritime colonies. While they escaped for a variety of reasons, such as family, autonomy, and mistreatment, the foundational reason was freedom. The quest for freedom should not blind historians to the fact that some runaways also used temporary escape as a way to negotiate for improved conditions *within* slavery such as more freedom to visit a relative or improved working circumstances. Historian Billy Smith captures this type of negotiation between slaveholders and female slaves, arguing that "some women [and, I would add, men] employed escape and other forms of resistance as bargaining devices to assert some control over their own lives and to curtail the power of their owners. This strategy might not gain their freedom, but it could improve the lives of slaves who desired a different master or wanted to live closer to kin and friends."[2]

1 The works mentioned here are important, but do not come close to listing all significant treatments of this subject. Antonio T. Bly, *Escaping Bondage: A Documentary History of Runaway Slaves in Eighteenth-Century New England, 1700–1789* (Lanham: Lexington, 2013); John Hope Franklin and Loren Schweninger, *Runaway Slaves: Rebels on the Plantation* (Oxford: Oxford UP, 1999); Billy G. Smith, "Black Women Who Stole Themselves in Eighteenth-Century America," in *Inequality in Early America*, ed. Carla Gardina Pestana and Sharon V. Salinger (Hanover: UP of New England, 1999), 134–59; David Waldstreicher, "Reading the Runaways: Self-Fashioning, Print Culture, and Confidence in Slavery in the Eighteenth-Century Mid-Atlantic," *William and Mary Quarterly* 56 (April 1999): 243–72; Amani Marshall, "'They Will Endeavor to Pass for Free': Enslaved Runaways' Performances of Freedom in Antebellum South Carolina," *Slavery and Abolition* 31 (June 2010): 161–80; Amani Marshall, "'They Are Supposed to Be Lurking about The City': Enslaved Women Runaways in Antebellum Charleston," *South Carolina Historical Magazine* 115 (July 2014): 188–212. Cornell University's important Freedom on the Move project is dedicated to runaway slaves (www.freedomonthemove.org).

2 Smith, "Black Women," 152.

DOCUMENT 1:

Halifax Slaves for Sale in Boston, Massachusetts, 1751[3]

This document shows that slaves were traded between New England and the Maritime colonies. These slaves were also highly skilled and extremely valuable to businessmen engaged in the seafaring industry and other economic pursuits.

JUST arriv'd from Hallifax, and to be sold, Ten hearty Strong Negro Men, mostly Tradesmen, such as Caulkers, Carpenters, Sailmakers, Ropemakers: Any Person inclining to purchase may enquire of Benjamin Hallowell of Boston.

3 *Boston Post Boy*, 23 September 1751.

DOCUMENT 2:
Slaves for Sale, Halifax, Nova Scotia, 1752[4]

In this document, Halifax merchant Joshua Mauger offered several slaves for sale in Nova Scotia. This suggests the existence of a viable local market in the region. Readers should pay attention to how Mauger described the work abilities of his slaves and also their ages.

Just imported, and to be sold by Joshua Mauger, at Major Lockman's store in Halifax, several Negro slaves, viz. A very likely Negro Wench, of about thirty five Years of Age, a **Creole born**, has been brought up in a Gentleman's family, and capable of doing all sorts of Work belonging thereto, as Needle-Work of all sorts, and in the best Manner; also Washing, Ironing, Cookery, and every other Thing that can be expected from Such a Slave. Also, 2 Negro boys of about 12 or 13 Years old, likely, healthy, and well shap'd, and understand some English: likewise 2 healthy Negro slaves of about 18 Years of Age, of agreable tempers, and fit for any kind of business; and also a healthy Negro Man of about 30 years of age.

Creole born: Born in the New World.

4 *Halifax Gazette*, 30 May 1752.

DOCUMENT 3:

Runaway Slave Advertisement, Female Slave Named Thursday, Nova Scotia, 1772[5]

The vast majority of runaway slaves in the Maritimes were young, usually single, and male. But, this broad truth should not hide the fact that many young women also absconded from their owners. Sometimes female runaways escaped with family members such as husbands and young children. In this case, Thursday attempted to run away from John Rock, but he recaptured her and ordered her sold in his 1776 will.

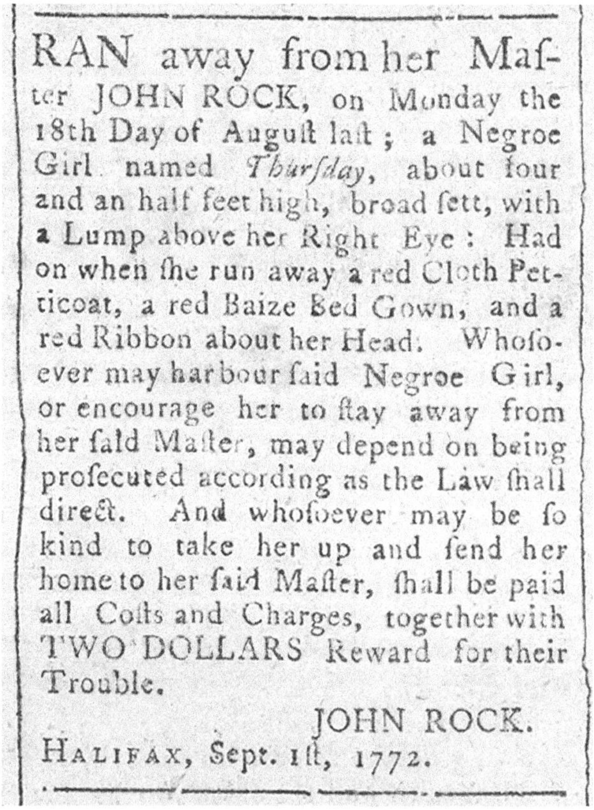

RAN away from her Maſter JOHN ROCK, on Monday the 18th Day of Auguſt laſt; a Negroe Girl named *Thurſday*, about four and an half feet high, broad ſett, with a Lump above her Right Eye: Had on when ſhe run away a red Cloth Petticoat, a red Baize Bed Gown, and a red Ribbon about her Head. Whoſoever may harbour ſaid Negroe Girl, or encourage her to ſtay away from her ſaid Maſter, may depend on being proſecuted according as the Law ſhall direct. And whoſoever may be ſo kind to take her up and ſend her home to her ſaid Maſter, ſhall be paid all Coſts and Charges, together with TWO DOLLARS Reward for their Trouble.

JOHN ROCK.

HALIFAX, Sept. 1ſt, 1772.

Fugitive slave advertisement in *Nova Scotia Gazette and Weekly Chronicle*, 1 September 1772, p. 3. Nova Scotia Archives Newspaper Collection: microfilm 8155.

5 *Nova Scotia Gazette and Weekly Chronicle*, 1 September 1772.

RAN away from her Master, JOHN ROCK, on Monday the 18th Day of August last; a Negroe Girl named *Thursday*, about four and an half feet high, broad sett, with a Lump above her Right Eye; Had on when she run away a red Cloth Petticoat, a red Baize Bed Gown, and a red Ribbon about her Head. Whosoever may harbour said Negroe Girl, or encourage her to stay away from her said Master, may depend on being prosecuted according as the Law shall direct. And whosoever may be so kind to take her up and send her home to her said master, shall be paid all Costs and Charges, together with TWO DOLLARS Reward for their Trouble.

JOHN ROCK

HALIFAX, Sept. 1, 1772.

DOCUMENT 4:
Slave Wanted Advertisement, Nova Scotia, 1776[6]

When people in the Maritimes wanted to purchase slaves, they usually waited for public auctions or for sale notices in local newspapers, but in this rare case a purchaser placed an advertisement describing the type of slave woman he wanted. Readers should note the purchaser's emphasis on his future slave's multi-occupational abilities.

WANTED, to purchase, A NEGRO WOMAN, about 25 or 30 years of Age, that understands cookery work and the management of a Dairy, she must be honest and bear a good character.—Enquire of the PRINTER.

6 *Royal Gazette*, 28 May 1776.

DOCUMENT 5:
Female Slave to Be Sold at Public Auction, Nova Scotia, 1783[7]

Readers should notice that the advertiser for this black woman did not even bother with her name, but rather just mentioned what type of slave work she could perform. During the 1780s and 1790s, Maritime slaves were sold at public auctions and through private transactions.

To be SOLD at PUBLIC AUCTION,
On Saturday the 28th Instant at the GOLDEN-BALL.
A Negro Wench, 25 Years of Age, a good House Servant.

7 *Nova Scotia Gazette and Weekly Chronicle*, 24 June 1783.

DOCUMENT 6:

Runaway Advertisement, James, Nova Scotia, 1781 and 1786[8]

Abel Michener's slave James absconded twice in five years. Readers should note the difference in tone between the first and second runaway notices. In the first one, the owner offered to forgive James if only he would come home. The second advertisement made no such offer of mercy. It is clear that James chose the clothes he took very carefully and this might be understood as a form of self-fashioning, which means the way in which runaway slaves used clothing to carve out a cultural or social space.

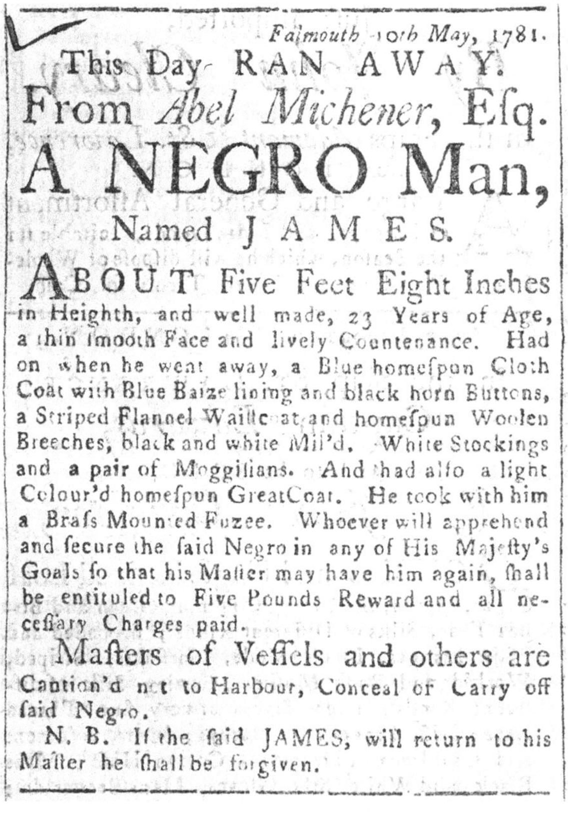

Falmouth 10th *May*, 1781.

This Day RAN AWAY.

From *Abel Michener*, Eſq.

A NEGRO Man,

Named J A M E S.

ABOUT Five Feet Eight Inches in Heighth, and well made, 23 Years of Age, a thin ſmooth Face and lively Countenance. Had on when he went away, a Blue homeſpun Cloth Coat with Blue Baize lining and black horn Buttons, a Striped Flannel Waiſtcoat and homeſpun Woolen Breeches, black and white Mill'd. White Stockings and a pair of Moggiſians. And had alſo a light Colour'd homeſpun GreatCoat. He took with him a Braſs Mounted Fuzee. Whoever will apprehend and ſecure the ſaid Negro in any of His Majeſty's Goals ſo that his Maſter may have him again, ſhall be entituled to Five Pounds Reward and all neceſſary Charges paid.

Maſters of Veſſels and others are Caution'd not to Harbour, Conceal or Carry off ſaid Negro.

N. B. If the ſaid JAMES, will return to his Maſter he ſhall be forgiven.

Runaway slave advertisement for "James," property of Abel Mitchener of Falmouth in *Nova Scotia Gazette*, 22 May 1781, p. 3. Nova Scotia Archives Newspaper Collection: microfilm 8159.

8 *Nova Scotia Gazette and Weekly Chronicle*, 22 May 1781 and 22 August 1786.

Falmouth 10th May 1781.
This Day RAN AWAY.
From *Abel Michener*, Esq.
A NEGRO Man,
Named JAMES.

ABOUT Five Feet Eight Inches in Heighth, and well made, 23 Years of Age, a thin smooth Face and lively Countenance. Had on when he went away, a Blue homespun Cloth Coat with Blue Baize lining and black horn Buttons, a Striped Flanel waistcoat and homespun Woolen Breeches, black and white Mil'd. White Stockings and a pair of Moggilians [type of shoes]. And had also a light Colour'd homespun Great Coat. He took with him a Brass Mounted Fuzee. Whoever will apprehend and secure the said Negro in any of His Majesty's [jails] that his Master may have him again, shall be entituled to Five **Pounds** Reward and all necessary Charges Paid.

Masters of Vessels and others are caution'd not to Harbour, Conceal or Carry off said Negro.

N.B. If the said JAMES, will return to his Master he shall be forgiven.

Pounds: The currency used in British America—pounds, shillings, pence, and guineas (one pound and one shilling). See the section on "Money and Slaves" in the Introduction.

Falmouth, 26th July, 1786
RAN away from the Subscriber on the 19th of this instant July, a NEGRO MAN, who answers to the Name of James about five feet eight Inches in heighth, 28 years of age, Smooth Face, a Nose rather acqueline, speaks good English, had on when he went a way a blue sear [?] Jacket, a Stripped flannel waistcoat, and [osnaburg] Trowsers, a black Hat, a Feather and Buckle, whoever will apprehend said Negro and return him to his Master, or secure him in any of his Majesty's [jails], so as that the Subscriber may have him again, shall have Forty Shillings Reward, and all reasonable Charges paid by.

Abel Michener,

N.B. Masters of Vessels, and all others are hereby [cautioned] against harbouring or carrying away said Negro.

DOCUMENT 7:

Runaway Slave Advertisement, An African Slave, Nova Scotia, 1783[9]

This runaway slave hailed from Africa, as indicated by his owner's description of his speech patterns and "Country marks" (ritual scarification among African ethnic groups). His owner, Hugh Kirkham, lived in South Carolina before the Revolutionary War, which makes sense as that region had engaged in mass importation of slaves from Africa during the eighteenth century. Readers should note the detailed description of Peter, which includes his speech patterns, strong evidence of African birth, age, and occupational skill.

HALIFAX, 8th May, 1783

RAN AWAY a smart Well looking Negro BOY named Peter, about Seventeen Years of Age: had On when he went a way a blue jacket, round hat, New Trousers of white Duck, new Shoes, and large plated buckles; he is round faced, speakes broken English, and when spoke to has a remarkable Smile on his Countenance, short and stout made, has been used to the carpenters business, and may attempt to pass for a free Man, this is [to?] warn all Masters of Vessels and Others not to harbor or Carry [off] said Negro as he is the property of the Subscriber; any one that will apprehend the said Negro so that his Master may receive him, Shall receive Eight Dollars Reward from

HUGH KIRKHAM

N.B. If he is stript he has his Country marks on his back in the form of a Square, thus.

Any Person harbouring or Concealing Said Boy will be prosecuted to the utmost rigor of the Law—if he returns of his Own Accord there will be nothing done to him.

9 *Nova Scotia Gazette and Weekly Chronicle*, 20 May 1783.

DOCUMENT 8:

Runaway Slave Advertisement, Dick, Nova Scotia, 1783[10]

This is a typical runaway advertisement. It does not tell us very much about Dick's occupation/work skill, speech patterns, character traits, or skin colour. It is possible that Dick either came from South Carolina, Georgia, or East Florida (where Ensign Douglass served with the King's Carolina Rangers). Douglass arrived with other refugees from East Florida in late 1783, so it seems that in the confusion following resettlement Dick took the opportunity to escape from his owner.

RUN away on the 27th inst. A Negro Man, named, Dick, (belonging to Mr. BENJAMIN DOUGLASS, late Ensign in the **King's Carolina Rangers**) about five feet eight inches high Stout Made, had on when he went away a red coat turn'd up with blue, white Waistcoat and Breeches, Aged about Twenty Seven Years. Whoever will apprehend Said Negro and bring him to Mr. ANDREW THOMSON, of *Halifax*, Merchant Shall be handsomely rewarded.

Nov. 29th, 1783.

King's Carolina Rangers: A regiment that fought several engagements during the Revolutionary War.

10 *Nova Scotia Gazette and Weekly Chronicle*, 9 December 1783.

DOCUMENT 9:

Runaway Slave Advertisement, Ben, Nova Scotia, 1783[11]

The Maritimes consist of interconnected ports which regularly had ships moving in and out of them in the 1780s and 1790s. Halifax, Saint John, and other towns must be understood as intimately connected ports of the wider Atlantic world through which commerce, trade, immigrants, and slaves traveled. In this advertisement, a ship's captain named John Smith bemoaned the escape of his "Negro lad" from his transport ship.

Two Guineas Reward
ABSCONTED himself on Thursday last from on Board the Transport Ship FRIENDS, a Negro Lad named Ben, he is 22 Years of Age, five feet four Inches high, of a remarkable dark complection Slender made, with a thin face and Large Lips, he has a Sore on one of his little fingers; and took with him three sailors Jackets and may pass for a Sailor. I hereby request all master of Vessels not to Ship him as he is my own property; and I forewarn any Person from harbouring or imploying him, as I shall [prosecute] them, who conceal him from me, and will give the above reward to them who may take him and bring him on board my Ship

John Wilson
Halifax, 12 May 1783

11 *Nova Scotia Gazette and Weekly Chronicle*, 20 May 1783.

DOCUMENT 10:

Slave for Sale, "Negro Boy," New Brunswick, 1784[12]

This slave for sale advertisement notes the slave's intelligence, personality type, age, and occupational skill. The advertisement says nothing about the boy's family, which probably means he was no longer in contact with them, or that his owner intended to sell him away from them.

TO BE SOLD
A Smart, active NEGRO BOY, about fifteen years of age, used to all kinds of household work, sold for no particular fault. Title Indisputable. For particulars enquire of the printers hereof.

12 *Saint John Gazette*, 15 July 1784.

DOCUMENT II:

Runaway Slave Advertisement, Hector, New Brunswick, 1784[13]

As this runaway advertisement shows, Hector lived throughout the Atlantic world. Because Hector is described as speaking like "West India negroes," it is likely that he was either born in Africa and/or had spent many of his formative years in the Caribbean. His owner Frederick William Hecht owned several slaves in New York before migrating to the Maritimes at the end of the Revolutionary War.

ult.: The previous month (short for *ultimo mense* [Latin]).

St. Augustine: St. Augustine is located on the northeastern coast of Florida. It was occupied at various times by both the Spanish and the British, including the Loyalists. It is located near Fort Mose, which was home to a settlement of free black people who served the Spanish Crown against British invasions in the eighteenth century.

Five Guineas Reward.
RUNAWAY from the subscriber, on Saturday evening the 26th **ult**. a negro man Slave, named Hector, by trade a cooper, a tall slender fellow, speaks English like the West India negroes, and is very talkative; he came from **St. Augustine** to this place, via New-York, on December last, had his feet frost bitten on the passage, and has a very lazy gait. Whoever secures and delivers him up to me shall have the above reward.

And as I have reason to suspect that he has been carried off by some vessel or other, I hereby offer the like reward to any person who can give information, so as the offender or offenders shall be convicted thereof.

Fred. Wm. Hecht.
Fort Howe, 13th July 1784

13 *Saint John Gazette*, 15 July 1784.

DOCUMENT 12:

Runaway Advertisement, Unfree Black Laborers, New Brunswick, 1784[14]

In the Maritimes, free people of African descent were prone to suffering re-enslavement at the hands of local whites who had promised to gainfully employ them and provide wages. For example, in July 1783 several free black people boarded the *Aurora* bound for the Saint John area. According to the **Book of Negroes**, Ed Morris (called Ned in BON, but his name seems to have been Edward), his wife Charity Morris, their three children (Isaac, Edward, and Mary Ann), and Peter Cox were free because the adults had **General Birch Certificates**, which was supposed to guarantee their liberty. Yet they were listed as being in the "possession" of Thomas Rogers.[15] The potential for re-enslavement among the Black Loyalists who migrated to the Maritimes was exacerbated because the Book of Negroes listed free blacks as being in the "possession" of a white Loyalist.[16] Obviously, this left black people vulnerable to re-enslavement or sale to the West Indies. Less than a year after their arrival, Thomas Rogers placed an unusually lengthy runaway notice complaining about the loss of his "Negroes" who he described as "belonging to the subscriber." In addition to the ones listed above, he also possessed Andrew Bush and his wife. This runaway advertisement demonstrates the lengths to which escaped unfree people were willing to go to obtain their freedom, but also how Rogers had taken away their freedom.

In his notice, Rogers identified one of the major difficulties facing Loyalist slaveholders, stating that "for the better security of indented servants, slaves, &c there [should be] a law of the province enacting that any person harbouring, concealing, or otherwise encouraging indented servants, apprentices or slaves from their master or their service, for every such offence shall forfeit the sum of ten pounds, &c." The problem, as Rogers saw it, rested on New Brunswick's failure to have enacted laws preventing local residents from protecting fugitive slaves and runaway indentured servants. Rogers also noted that "a certain Mr. Dibble, has encouraged some of the aforesaid servants." Apparently, Dibble had told Rogers' unfree black servants to lodge a complaint with local magistrates, "to have them liberated," but it failed mostly due to **John Coffin** who "judiciously" decided in Rogers' favour. Without question, Edward Morris, his wife, and the other unfree labourers

Book of Negroes: A list of thousands of African Americans who left the American colonies for the Maritimes, Quebec, and other regions throughout the British Empire at the conclusion of the Revolutionary War (1783). Although the majority of names in the Book of Negroes are those who obtained their freedom during the war, it also contains the names of slaves. The document includes an individual black person's name, age, sex, and a description of how they came to British lines. Once under British protection, most former slaves were given General Birch Certificates (GBC) denoting their freedom. Often, historians have used the Book of Negroes to examine the Black Loyalists or those who gained freedom during the Revolution, but it also includes the names of hundreds of Loyalist slaves.

General Birch Certificates: Certificates of freedom given to black people at the end of the Revolutionary War which allowed the holder of the document to go where he/she pleased.

John Coffin: From an elite family in Boston, Coffin fought in several engagements throughout the Revolutionary War including Bunker Hill. After the war, Coffin settled in New Brunswick where he became a successful businessman, judge, and politician.

14 *Royal Saint John's Gazette* (Saint John), 13 May 1784.

15 Book of Negroes, Sir Guy Carleton Papers, National Archives (UK), microfilm copy at Nova Scotia Archives.

16 Carole Watterson Troxler, "Uses of the Bahamas by Southern Loyalist Exiles," in *The Loyal Atlantic: Remaking the British Atlantic in the Revolutionary Era*, ed. Liam Riordan and Jerry Bannister (Toronto: U of Toronto P, 2012), 200.

were quite capable of wanting their freedom without encouragement from Dibble, but certainly his help would have been appreciated.

Although these runaways had General Birch Certificates, Rogers claimed that they were unfree labourers. In less than one year from their arrival in New Brunswick, they had gone from free black Loyalists to unfree indentured servants and the next step easily could have been enslavement (if they were not already being treated as slaves). Reflecting on white treatment of free blacks, African American Baptist preacher David George noted that "White people in Nova Scotia" had "treated many of us as bad as though we (free blacks) had been slaves" (see Document 48). Edward Morris, his wife Charity, their child, Peter Cock, Andrew Bush, and his wife had lost their freedom and were being treated as David George noted, that is, like slaves—despite their legal status as free. They absconded from Rogers because he had deprived them of their freedom and planned to do worse such as break up their families through sale. Perhaps these people realized that they were about to be re-enslaved by an unscrupulous master or sold to the West Indies and this is precisely why they absconded as a group. It was rather common for white Loyalists not to pay wages they owed to black workers—in effect re-enslaving them.

It is certainly plausible that Rogers had turned them into *de facto* slaves by not paying any wages, and this might have resulted in their decision to abscond. Another possible reason behind their escape is that Rogers might have taken and sold some of their children. Charity Morris had three children when she left New York in 1783.[17] But by May 1784 the runaway notice only mentions one of her children with Edward Morris. What happened to the other two? Had they died earlier in the winter or did Rogers illegally sell them to the West Indies? Black children were at extreme risk for re-enslavement and, without the intervention of the local authorities, they could easily be sold to the West Indies (see Document 48, p. 86).

At best, Thomas Rogers' servants' potential freedom was extremely precarious, while their *de facto* enslavement seems rather likely. Slaves and indentured black servants regularly married and ran away together, underlining the similarity of their status and the dangerous situation they confronted in a society that sometimes allowed their sale to the West Indies. The prevention of black people being sold out of the region as slaves depended almost wholly on the government's willingness to enforce certain laws and black people's ability to escape. In escaping from Rogers, his "servants" were asserting their freedom and autonomy. Rogers' runaway advertisement also illuminates the

17 Book of Negroes.

social disorder that could occur between anti-slavery whites and those who supported black bondage. Mr. Dibble seemingly wanted to provide some sort of escape for the Morris family and their companions. The runaways did not accept Rogers' claims and they escaped only to have their master prevail upon the court system to have them returned to him. Yet they absconded again. Although there were multiple reasons for their escape, Rogers' black unfree labourers wanted their liberty and were willing to try different types of escape to break free of his suffocating grasp.

HARBOURED, or otherwise CONCEALED,

THE following Negroes belonging to the subscriber, viz. Edward Morris, an elderly negro about five feet five inches high, by trade a mason, has a remarkable wound in his forehead which shews a hole resembling a bullet shot, is a celebrated methodist preacher among the negroes, was bred at Fairfield in Connecticut; also Charity his wife, a half bred Indian of the tribe on Long Island, province of New York, and a small boy about eleven years of age, son of the said wench by an Indian father.

Andrew Bush, a **comely** stout negro, remarkable high forwarded, generally called the **Widow's Peek,** formerly the property of Doctor Bush in Connecticut, is a remarkable good miller, which practice he has been used all his life to, also his wife Eanus, a **yellow mustee**.

And Peter Cock, a young negro, comely countenance, **bandy** with one leg, and has spent best part of the last six months at the house and in the neighbourhood of a person named White Raymond, in or near the lower cove, at Parr.

N.B. The subscriber thinks it his duty to apprize the public that for the better security of indented servants, slaves, & c. there is a law of the province enacting, that any person harbouring, concealing, or otherwise encouraging indented servants, apprentices or slaves from their master or their service, for every such offence shall forfeit the sum of ten pounds, & c. And whereas the subscriber is well informed that a certain Mr. Dibble, has encouraged some of the aforesaid servants, and as he is determined, however secure said Mr. Dibble may suppose himself by virtue of his commission of the peace, assures the public, however exalted the person, that he is determined on putting the laws in force against said Dibble: And as he said Mr. Dibble, after taking great pains to council and recommend the subscriber's servants, by lodging a [vexatious] complaint before three Magistrates, in hopes by such complaint to have them liberated, but failing in this, for which the peculiar thanks of

comely: Attractive.

Widow's Peek: Widow's peak—a V-shaped receding hairline, usually in men.

yellow mustee: An octoroon, i.e., a person of mixed racial ancestry. Europeans devised a classification system of mixed race people ranging from "mulatto" (a person with one African and one European parent or two parents of mixed race) to "quadroon" (a person with one-quarter African ancestry) to "octoroon" (a person with one-eighth African ancestry). These ideas were based on the specious notion that race should define and decide one's place in society.

bandy: Bow-legged.

the subscriber is due to John Coffin, Esq; for his impartiality in hearing and judiciously determining the same to be false, [vexatious] and groundless, has endeavoured, by various means and arts, to become a proprietor of said subscriber's indebt'd servants, under pretence of purchasing them, but which subscriber hereby, as he has done before, informs him, [and] Dibble, that he will not have any bargain, or other negociation whatever touching the above servants, and hereby once more forwarns him from farther harbouring, concealing, or otherwise preventing said negroes from returning to their duty, under penalty of the law in such case provided.

And the subscriber, tenacious of doing an injury to any individual who has innocently, and unaware of the above penalty, employed any of the aforesaid deserters, most particularly submits the danger of such conduct to their serious consideration, and hopes for their readiness in apprehending and returning to the said proprietor the above indented persons, and in particular the gentlemen who are well known to the subscriber, who for some months past, at Maugerville, have employed the above mentioned Andrew Bush and Eanus his wife, which will be acknowledged with gratitude, the contrary will be deemed injurious to the party, and recompence will be sought accordingly.

THOMAS ROGERS

DOCUMENT 13:
Runaway Slave Advertisement, Jupiter and Clarinda, Nova Scotia, 1784[18]

A Loyalist from South Carolina, Nathaniel Bullern (Bullen or Bullein) arrived in Nova Scotia with ten slaves. In the following runaway notice, he complained about the loss of, "TWO NEGRO—the Property of Mr. Nath. Bullern, the One an indented Servant, the Other a Slave." These two people, servant and slave, were both part of a world of "unfreedom." In running away together, they saw their status as similar if not the same. Jupiter and Clarinda had both arrived in Nova Scotia as slaves, but shortly after arrival Bullern had freed one of them. In the Book of Negroes, Clarinda (age 19) and Jupiter (age 33) are listed one after the other. Clarinda seems to have been the property of Henry Boyd before becoming the property of Dr. Bullern.

RUN AWAY 8th September
TWO NEGRO—the Property of Mr. Nath Bullern, the One an [indented] Servant, the other a Slave; the Man had on when he went away a [?] Hatt, a blue Coat, about 6 feet high, answered to the name of JUPITER—The woman had on a short red Bays Bedgown, answers to the name Clarinda. Whoever will apprehend the same, and bring to Mr. Robert Spicer, at Fort Needham, near Halifax, shall receive 20 Shillings Reward.
N.B. Whoever takes away the same out of Halifax either by Sea or Land, will be sued for the same.

18 *Nova Scotia Gazette and Weekly Chronicle*, 21 September 1784.

DOCUMENT 14:
A Family Escapes, Nova Scotia, 1785[19]

In this document, James and his family ran away from their owner Samuel Andrews. Although James would have stood a much better chance of escaping alone, his entire family accompanied him. This is a testament to the importance of family bonds among slaves in the Maritimes and the United States. Andrews probably recaptured the family and in 1800 he and his sons murdered a female slave named Jude or Judy (probably the same child listed in this slave advertisement, see Document 64, p. 116).

RUN AWAY from the Subscriber

Four Negroes,
A Man, his Wife, and two Children, [named] *James*, *Bet*, *Frank*, and *Judy*, who all speak good English; the man is a carpenter by trade. WHOEVER apprehends the said negroes, and delivers them to the gaol keeper, or to Capt. John William, in Maiden-lane, shall receive EIGHT DOLLARS Reward, or any person that will give information to said Williams, of said negroes, so that he gets hold of them, shall receive a Reward of FIVE DOLLARS from Said Williams.
SAMUEL ANDREWS

19 *Nova Scotia Packet and General Advertiser*, 12 October 1785.

DOCUMENT 15:

Slave for Sale Advertisement, 14-Year-Old, Nova Scotia, 1786[20]

In this sale notice, the owner leaves an impressive description of his young teenage male slave. He was a multi-occupational slave responsible for a variety of tasks. In this sense, he was very similar to other slaves in northeastern North America in that he did not work in a staple-producing state like South Carolina.

TO BE SOLD

A Healthy Stout, NEGRO BOY, about fourteen Years of Age.—He has been brought up in a Gentleman's Family, is very handy at Farming, House-Work, or attending Table, is strictly honest, and has an exceeding good Temper. For Particulars, enquire of the Printer.

20 *Royal American Gazette*, 19 June 1786.

DOCUMENT 16:

Slave for Sale Advertisement, 14-Year-Old Boy, New Brunswick, 1786[21]

In this document, James Hayt offers for sale a young teenage slave. Readers should note Hayt's wording that the slave would be useful "in a family." This phrasing acknowledged the fact that many slaves in the Maritimes were part of what historians have called family slavery, which meant that African American slaves worked next to their owners, ate with them, and slept in the same houses. This proximity made slaves part of the household and family they served, but this was not necessarily a positive development because it did not easily allow slaves to develop an independent community with other slaves as they could in, for example, a large-scale plantation in South Carolina.

JAMES HAYT,
HAS FOR SALE,
A BLACK BOY, fourteen years of age, in full vigor of health, very active, has a pleasing countenance and every ability to render himself useful and agreeable in a family. The title for him is indisputable.

21 *Royal Gazette*, 12 September 1786.

DOCUMENT 17:

Slaves for Sale Advertisement, A Man and Boy, New Brunswick, 1786[22]

In this document, the local sheriff held a public auction of the property of a local innkeeper named Charles McPherson. His property included two unnamed slaves. We do not know if these two people were father and son or possibly unrelated. Readers should note how two human beings are placed on the same level as birch boards and empty gin cases: all are simply items to be sold.

TO BE SOLD AT PUBLIC AUCTION
At the EXCHANGE COFFEE HOUSE, in this city, on Monday next, at 12 O'CLOCK at noon:

FORTY-SIX hogsheads of London Porter; 2 hogsheads, 4 casks and a box of bottled Ale ... Tables, Chairs, Benches, Looking Glasses, Clock and Case, Beds and Bedsteads, Pictures, Glass Lamps, Sconces....

ALSO, a NEGRO MAN and BOY, a Sloop rigged vessel, with mast, bowsprit, Sails, &c. a Waggon, Birch Boards, empty Gin Cases, and a variety of other articles too tedious to mention. Late the property of CHARLES McPHERSON, Inn-holder, seized and taken in execution by W.S. Oliver, Sheriff.
St. John, July 4, 1786

22 *Royal Gazette*, 4 July 1786.

DOCUMENT 18:

Runaway Slave Advertisement, Ben, New Brunswick, 1786[23]

In this advertisement, Ben escapes from Captain Caleb Jones. He would soon be recaptured, and would later the same year attempt another escape with several slaves (see Document 19, p. 47).

Five Dollars Reward

RUN away, a negro man named BEN, about thirty years of age, the property of Capt. Jones, had on when he went away a light brown jacket, a plad waistcoat, corduroy breeches, white stockings, and a round hat; is about five feet six inches high, stout and well set, has very black thick lips. Whoever takes up the said negro and delivers him to James Moore near Fredericton, or, secures him that the owner may get him again, shall have the above reward, and all reasonable charges paid.

23 *Royal Gazette*, 7 March 1786.

DOCUMENT 19:

Runaway Slave Advertisement, Five Slaves Escape Caleb Jones, New Brunswick, 1786[24]

In this runaway advertisement, five of Caleb Jones' slaves attempted to escape from their brutal owner. The fact that five of his slaves ran away underlines the extent of their suffering. We don't know exactly what caused this specific incident of running away, but the fact that the entire group left shows that Jones had done something that they all saw as objectionable. Jones was one of the most important slaveholders in Loyalist New Brunswick. He participated in the famous "Nancy" case in 1800, which resulted in his slave being returned to him (see Document 62, p. 114). In 1816, Lidge attempted to escape again from Caleb Jones—30 years after this escape attempt (see Document 40, p. 70).

RAN AWAY

FROM the subscriber living at the **Nashwakshis**, in the county of York, between the 15th and 21st days of this instant July [June?], the following bound Negro slaves, viz., ISAAC about 30 years old, born on Long Island near New-York, had on when he went away, a short blue coat, round hat and white trowsers. BEN, about 35 years old, had on a **Devonshire Kersey** jacket lined with Scotch plad, corduroy breeches, and round hat. FLORA, a wench about 27 years old, much pitted with the small-pox, she had on a white cotton jacket and petticoat. ALSO NANCY about 24 years old, who took with her a Negro child, about four years old called LIDGE. The four last mentioned Negroes were born in Maryland, and lately brought to this country.

Nashwakshis: A village near Fredericton, New Brunswick.

Devonshire Kersey: A coarse woollen cloth.

All Person are hereby forbid to harbour any of the above Negroes, and all masters of vessels are forbid to take any of them on board their vessel as they shall answer the consequences. A REWARD of TWO GUINEAS, will be paid for each of the men, and SIX DOLLARS for each Negro woman, by Mr. THOMAS JENNINGS, if taken and deliver'd to him at the City of Saint John, at York Point, and if taken any where else and deliver'd to the said JENNINGS, or to the Subscriber in York County, the like reward with all reasonable charges will be paid by the said JENNINGS or the subscriber.

CALEB JONES.

24 June 1786.

24 *Royal Gazette*, 25 July 1786.

DOCUMENT 20:

Runaway Slave Advertisement, Dinah, Nova Scotia, 1786[25]

In this document, a single young woman escaped on her own from Robert Wilkins.

Five Dollars Reward
RUNAWAY from the subscriber, on Saturday, the 22nd Instant, a NEGRO WENCH, named DINAH, about twenty five Years of Age; had on when she went away, a blue and white Ticking Petticoat, a purple and white Callico short Gown, and an old blue Cloak.—Whoever will apprehend and secure said Wench, so that the Owner may have her again, shall receive the above Reward, with reasonable Charges.

ROBERT WILKINS.

Shelburne, Mowat Street, July 24, 1786

Masters of Vessels and Others are hereby forbid to carry off or harbour said Wench, at their Peril.

25 *Nova Scotia Packet and General Advertiser*, 3 August 1786.

DOCUMENT 21:

Slave for Sale Advertisement, Teenage Girl, New Brunswick, 1787[26]

If owners did not want their slaves, they could try to sell them and diversify their economic portfolio. The owner, Thomas Mallard, wanted to sell a good country/farm slave, but the fact that he did not emphasize her domestic skills (cooking, washing, cleaning) might have turned off potential buyers who wanted a domestic or household slave.

TO BE SOLD
A Likely, healthy negro wench, of about 17 years of age, is well calculated for the country, and sold for want of employ.—The title indisputable. If not sold within 8 days from the date hereof by private sale, she will sold at public auction.—Enquire of THOMAS MALLARD.

26 *Royal Gazette*, 11 September 1787.

DOCUMENT 22:

Slave for Sale Advertisement, Young Woman, New Brunswick, 1787[27]

This advertisement describes a typical household slave and her occupational skills to potential buyers.

To be SOLD,
A WENCH about 23 years old, is well acquainted with all kinds of household business, and particular is an excellent COOK.—To be disposed of for no fault, but want of employ.—Enquire as above

27 *Royal Gazette*, 21 August 1787.

DOCUMENT 23:

Runaway Slave Advertisement, Sam and Beller (siblings) Escape, New Brunswick, 1787[28]

In this runaway notice, three black people escaped from Thomas Lester. Two of them, Sam and Beller, were siblings and Lester seems to have owned them from an early age. The free man, Tony Smith, who escaped with them underlines the point that there might not have been much difference between the way black servants and slaves were treated by their masters or employers. In this case, Smith ran off with two people whose legal status was far worse than his, but he seemed to make common cause with them.

RUN-AWAY

IN a BIRCH CANOE, from the subscriber two negro Men and one Wench; who have taken sundry things with them. SAM, between a black and dark **Mulatto** 17 or 18 years old, midling tall and slim; quick spoken, attempts to play the VIOLIN, has a London brown coloured coat, ticking trousers and other clothes.

BELLER, a sister to SAM, between a black and mulatto, 16 years old, midling tall and slim, is raw bon'd has a scar between her eye and temple, is slow in her speech, has a black cover'd hat with white lining, and lived formerly with Judge Peters[29] at Saint John.

TONY SMITH, some call him JOE, a free fellow, but hired for a time; he is tall and slim, between a black and mulatto, speaks broken, wears blue or brown coat, ticking trousers, and has other clothes with him.—Two of the above servants were raised in the family. Any person apprehending them or giving information to Mr. EZRA SCOFIELD, in King Street, St. John, or the subscriber, shall have One GUINEA for each, and if taken out of St. John, reasonable charges paid—if taken out of the province, it is requested that they may be confined in Jail until called for. All masters of vessels and every other person is forwarned not to carry any of the said negroes off or from harbouring or concealing them, as they will answer it at their peril.

THOMAS LESTER

Waterborough, 19th June 1787

Mulatto: This term meant a person with mixed-race ancestry (usually one white and one black parent, but also possibly two parents of mixed heritage). Some scholars view this term as being derived from the word "mule"; the actual origin is not completely clear, though some scientific racists of the nineteenth century tried to claim that mixed race people were sterile like mules.

28 *Royal Gazette*, 10 July 1787.

29 Judge Peters was another slaveholder. Presumably this is the same person who bequeathed slaves to his relatives. See Will of James Peters, 1821, Provincial Archives of New Brunswick, Fredericton, New Brunswick.

DOCUMENT 24:

Runaway Slave Advertisement, Abraham, Teenager, New Brunswick, 1787[30]

Although only 16 years of age, Abraham had already had two or more owners. We know nothing about his parents or other family members and how long he may have been separated from them. James Hayt owned several slaves and his advertisement seems to indicate a deep fondness for young Abraham—note his description of Abraham's physical appearance.

SIXTEEN DOLLARS REWARD,
AND all reasonable charges will be paid by James Hayt, to any person who will detect and return ABRAHAM, a Run-Away negro boy, about 16 years of age—he had on a short blue jacket, with sleeves lined with white swan skin, a scarlet waistcoat, two rows bright buttons, with a collar, nankeen breeches, thread stockings, new shoes, plated buckles, and [an] all round black hat.—He has a pleasant countenance, is very talkative, tall of his age, but well proportioned, and formerly belonged to Capt. John Hall, of Saint Andrews. JAMES HAYT
September 12th, 1787.

30 *Royal Gazette*, 12 October 1787.

DOCUMENT 25:

Runaway Slave Advertisement, London, Age 18, New Brunswick, 1787[31]

This brief runaway notice does not tell historians much about London aside from his age. However, his master Joseph Clarke owned several slaves and also was part of an important court case about slavery (see Document 30, p. 58 and Document 67, p. 119).

RAN AWAY from the subscriber, the 19th of July last, LONDON, a negro boy, aged 18 years, had on when he went away a light colored coating jacket, osnaburg trowsers, green bay shirt, with white sleeves, and wants the first joint of the second toe of the left foot. Whoever will apprehend the said negro and secure him, so that his master, may get him again, shall have ONE GUINEA Reward; and all masters of vessels and others are hereby forbid to carry him off, or to employ him as a servant or otherwise.

JOSEPH CLARKE

31 *Royal Gazette*, 17 August 1787.

DOCUMENT 26:
Runaway Slave Advertisement, Keziah, New Brunswick, 1787[32]

In this runaway advertisement, Thomas Bean's description of his slave Keziah offers the careful reader an insight into how this woman wanted to "self-fashion" (this means that slaves were interested in projecting an image of how they wanted the world to see them) her appearance through apparel. The amount of clothing she took with her is stunning. The scarification on her face might indicate that Keziah was born in Africa before she was brought to New Brunswick.

RUN-AWAY

FROM the subscriber, on Wednesday evening last the 15th instant, a negro woman named KEZIAH, about five feet high, has the marks of a cut and a burn, I believe, on her right cheek, near her mouth, took with her two calico gowns, the one a white, the other a **nankeen** ground, the flowers running through it in stripes, also, a dark purple and white calico frisk and petticoat—has different short gowns, among which is a blue and white striped linen, and a white: Also, a white cloth cloak and a black bonnet lined with white, covered with gauze, and lace hooped round the edge.—Whoever will apprehend and take up said negro woman, so that her master may have her again, shall receive a reward of TWO GUINEAS, and all reasonable charges paid.

All Masters of vessels and others are hereby forbid carrying off the said Negro slave, as they will answer for it at their peril.

Aug. 17th THOMAS BEAN.

nankeen: A cotton cloth of a yellowish colour originally made in China, but by the time of this advertisement mostly made out of cotton and dyed yellow in Manchester, England. See Kathleen A. Staples and Madelyn Shaw, *Clothing through American History: The British Colonial Era* (Santa Barbara: Greenwood, 2013), 420.

32 *Royal Gazette*, 21 August 1787.

DOCUMENT 27:

Slave for Sale Advertisement, Young Black Woman, New Brunswick, 1788[33]

In this advertisement, the owner offers a young woman for sale. He describes her personality and also notes that she had been previously owned.

FOR SALE,
A Stout, **likely** and very active Young BLACK WOMAN, late the property of John H Carey; she is not offered for any fault, but is singularly sober and diligent.—Enquire of James Hayt.
October 3, 1788

likely: The slave was valuable or would become valuable.

33 *Saint John Gazette*, 16 January 1789.

DOCUMENT 28:

Runaway Slave Advertisement, Prince, New Brunswick, 1788[34]

Readers should compare this advertisement with John Agnew's runaway notice (Document 31, p. 60). This might be the same Prince.

Three POUNDS REWARD

RUN-AWAY, last night, a negro man named PRINCE, a stout well made fellow, about five feet eight inches high, has a sour down look; had on and took with him, a new blanket coat, a red short jacket, (the laps faced with green,) an old drab coating, a corduroy pair breeches, an old pair coating trowsers, two new check shirts, one new pair of shoes, one pair half boots, 2 black caps, one dog and the other bear skin, and one white hat.—WHOEVER will secure him in any jail in this province, or bring him to his master near Fredericton, shall have the above reward, and all reasonable charges.

May 20th 1788

Benj. Davis

N.B. All Masters of vessels are forbid carrying him off, and all persons from harbouring or employing the above described fellow.

34 *Royal Gazette*, 17 June 1788.

DOCUMENT 29:

Runaway Slave Advertisement, Poll, New Brunswick, 1791[35]

This document is another example of an enslaved runaway female. The advertisement does not tell us much about her aside from her age and the fact she had suffered from smallpox.

Four Dollars Reward.
RUNAWAY from the subscriber on FRIDAY the 26th instant, a Negro Wench named Poll, about 17 years of age, very much pitted with the small pox.—[Whoever] takes up said Wench and delivers her to the subscriber shall receive the above reward.

ALEXANDER MORTON

N.B. All Masters of vessels are forbid taking off said WENCH; all persons are forbid harbouring her [as they] may depend upon being prosecuted with the utmost rigour of the Law.
St. John, Aug. 30, 1791

35 *Saint John Gazette*, 30 September 1791.

DOCUMENT 30:

Runaway Slave Advertisement, Statia and Her Family, New Brunswick, 1792[36]

Statia and Dick were escaping to protect their family from their predatory master Joseph Clarke. They probably feared he would break apart the family and prevent the couple from being together. Clarke recaptured the runaways and then immediately sold Statia to another man, which resulted in her being separated from her husband and children. The case of Statia did not end there, as her son became part of an important legal case 13 years later (see Document 67, p. 119).

Three Guineas Reward

RAN-AWAY

FROM the Subscriber on the night of the 9th instant, an indented servant Man, named

DICK HOPEWELL;

about 5 feet 9 inches high—very active, and supposed to be near 40 years of age.—Had on when he went off a **fearnought** grey short coat and trowsers with white metal buttons—a new felt hat, & c.

fearnought: Thick woollen material.

At the same time went off a Negro Woman slave, named

STATIA,

who he claim'd as a Wife, with two small children—a boy about 5 years old, and a girl about 15 months—she is about 30 years of age, and now pregnant.—Had on when she went off a green duffle petticoat, with a baize short gown of the same colour—she is of the mulatto cast, and speaks very fluently.—Whoever will secure said RUN-AWAYS in any gaol of this Province, or the Province of Nova-Scotia, so that their master may recover them, shall be entitled to the above reward.

---

36 *Saint John Gazette*, 29 June 1792.

MASTERS of vessels and others are hereby cautioned not to harbour, conceal or employ said RUN-AWAYS, as they will be prosecuted to the utmost rigour of the Law.

JOSEPH CLARKE.
Maugerville, 14th *June*, 1792.

DOCUMENT 31:

Runaway Slave Advertisement, Prince, New Brunswick, 1792[37]

This remarkable runaway notice is one of the most descriptive we have of an individual slave in terms of his clothing and personality traits. As stated earlier, slaves carefully chose their clothing and this can be understood as a form of self-fashioning. We must remember that slaves, like people today, had various fashion tastes that informed their ideas of themselves. We cannot deny that slavery was incredibly oppressive, but this should not lead us to the false conclusion that slaves had no agency in the making of their own lives. They made the best of their lives and we should not dehumanize them to the point that we deny their obvious examples of self-expression—clothing gives us an avenue to consider this aspect of slave history.

RUNAWAY
FROM THE SUBSCRIBER, on the 4th inst. A NEGRO MAN Slave named PRINCE.—He carried off with him a new grey cloth coat with short skirts, and a lapelled waistcoat, and trowsers of the same, all neatly made, and mounted with metal buttons—also a new [?] coat of a lighter grey, with metal buttons and long skirts—a new fox skin cap with a bushy tail, and a good hat—three good shirts—one of them stout linen—a pair of good shoes, and a pair of new grey and purple colored stockings, and a very good blue and black coloured coat, mounted with silk chequered buttons, rather too large for him.

He is artful, has a gloomy and malevolent look—is a daring liar, and has attempted twice before this to RUN-AWAY.

ALL masters of vessels and others are hereby warned against carrying said NEGRO out of the Province, entertaining, harbouring, or employing him in any manner—and whoever takes and secures said NEGRO in any GAOL in this Province, and gives information to Messrs. Thomson & Reid, Merchants, *St. John*, or the SUBSCRIBER in Maugerville, so that his master can recover him, shall be handsomely REWARDED.
JOHN AGNEW.
Maugerville, 5 May 1792.

---

37 *Saint John Gazette*, 29 June 1792.

DOCUMENT 32:

Runaway Slave Advertisement, Joseph Odel and Peter Lawrence, Nova Scotia, 1792[38]

In this advertisement, two black men ran off from their owners in **Digby**. They might have attempted to get on board a vessel as ship hands because that would have gotten them out of the area and also provided them with wages.

Digby: A town located on the coast of southwestern Nova Scotia where numerous Loyalist slaveholders and slaves settled. See Digby slaveholder petition (Document 53, p. 93).

DIGBY, 21st June 1792

RUN AWAY, Joseph Odel and Peter Lawrence (Negroes) from their Masters, and left Digby last evening, the first mentioned is about Twenty four year of Age, five feet six Inches high, had on a light brown coat, red waistcoat and thickset breeches, took other cloaths with him, he is a likely young Fellow with remarkable white Teeth.—The other is about five Feet eight Inches high, very Black, had on lightesh coloured Clothes.—Whoever will secure said Negroes so that their Masters may have them again, shall receive TEN DOLLARS Reward, and all reasonable Charges paid.
DANIEL ODEL
PHILLIP EARL

38 *Royal Gazette*, 10 July 1792.

DOCUMENT 33:

Runaway Slave Advertisement, Bill/Belfast, Nova Scotia, 1794[39]

Slaves escaped for a variety of reasons including mistreatment, the desire for freedom, or the possibility of negotiating improved conditions within slavery if they were recaptured. Running away left a powerful impression on slaveholders, and the shrewd ones who recaptured their slaves knew if they wanted to continue to benefit from their slave's labour, they had to make concessions or face another runaway attempt. On the other hand, slaves like Bill knew the possibilities and pitfalls of absconding. As a result, Bill carefully planned his escape down to the very last detail. His owner Michael Wallace left an incredibly detailed portrait of Bill in this runaway notice. The slave notice shows two men, one using the coercion of slavery and the other using the weapons of the powerless—his wit and craftiness—struggling to gain the upper hand over one another. Readers should note how carefully Bill planned his escape by having clothes hidden throughout Halifax.

Twenty Dollars Reward

RAN Away, on Thursday evening, the 18th inst. a Negro Man Servant, the property [of the] Subscriber, named Belfast; but who commonly goes by the name of Bill.———— At the time of the elopement he was in the service of William Forsyth, Esq; and had meditated an attempt to get on board a ship that night which lay in the harbour, bound to Newfoundland; but was frustrated: It is probable, however, he may still endeavor to escape that way, therefore, the masters of all coasters going along shore, or other vessels bound to sea, are hereby forewarned from carrying him off at their peril, as they will be prosecuted, if discovered, with the utmost rigour of the law.

The above reward will be paid to any person or persons who shall apprehend and secure him, so that I may recover him again.

He is a likely, stout-made fellow, of five feet eight or nine inches high, and about 27 years of age; of a mild good countenance and features, smooth black skin, with very white teeth; is a native of South Carolina, speaks good English, and very softly, and has been in this province for ten years.

Bath-Coating: "A thick, double-raised baise [a woollen cloth] used for overcoats." See Valerie Cumming, C.W. Cunnington, P.E. Cunnington, *The Dictionary of Fashion History* (New York: Berg, 2010), 232.

When he went off, he wore an old **Bath-Coating** short coat, of a light colour, wore out at the elbows; brown cloth or [duffle?] trowsers, also much wore at the knees; a round hat, and an old black silk handkerchief about his

39 *Weekly Chronicle*, 15 March 1794.

neck:—But as he had other cloaths secreted in town, he may have changed his whole apparel.

He will no doubt endeavour to pass for a free man, and possibly by some other name.

MICHAEL WALLACE.

Twenty Dollars Reward.

RAN Away, on Thurſday evening, the 18th inſt. a Negro Man Servant, the property of the Subſcriber, named BELFAST; but who commonly goes by the name of BILL.———At the time of he elopement he was in the ſervice of William Forſyth, Eſq; and had meditated an attempt to get on board a ſhip that night which lay in the harbour, bound to Newfoundland; but was fruſtrated: It is probable, however, he may ſtill endeavour to eſcape that way, therefore, the maſters of all coaſters going along ſhore, or other veſſels bound to ſea, are hereby forewarned from carrying him off at their peril, as they will be proſecuted, if diſcovered, with the utmoſt rigour of the law.

The above reward will be paid to any perſon or perſons who ſhall apprehend and ſecure him, ſo that I may recover him again.

He is a likely, ſtout-made fellow, of five feet eight or nine inches high, and about 27 years of age; of a mild good countenance and features, ſmooth black ſkin, with very white teeth; is a native of South Carolina, ſpeaks good Engliſh, and very ſoftly, and has been in this Province ten years.

When he went off, he wore an old Bath-Coating ſhort coat, of a light colour, wore out at the elbows; brown cloth or duffil trowſers, alſo much wore at the knees; a round hat, and an old black ſilk handkerchief about his neck:—But as he had other cloaths ſecreted in town, he may have changed his whole apparel.

He will no doubt endeavour to paſs for a free man, and poſſibly by ſome other name.

MICHAEL WALLACE.

Runaway slave advertisement in *Weekly Chronicle*, 15 March 1794, p. 1. Nova Scotia Archives Newspaper Collection: microfilm 8165.

DOCUMENT 34:

Slave for Sale, Young Man, New Brunswick, 1799[40]

This is a typical slave for sale advertisement. This male slave was multi-occupational and could work on farms and within the household. Most slaves in the Maritimes were able to do various tasks ranging from farm labour to urban work to domestic service.

TO BE SOLD,

A NEGRO MAN, about 20 years of age—is short, but well made, and very active—can do all sorts of Farming work, and is a handy House Servant.—For terms &c. enquire of Mr. Ryan.

Saint John, 11th June, 1799.

40 *Royal Gazette*, 11 June 1799.

DOCUMENT 35:

Runaway Slave Advertisement, Gill and Dick, New Brunswick, 1799[41]

Gill and Dick decided to abscond together. No doubt they believed that the comfort of being with another runaway would offset their fear of capture. They were owned by different men, so the fact they ran away together indicates that black slaves in the Maritimes were able to establish friendships and communities outside of their households. Both men took extra clothing, which demonstrates that they had carefully considered their escape and wanted to make sure they had enough apparel to keep warm on cool nights.

Five Guineas Reward
RANAWAY on Sunday the 11th instant, two Negro Men named GILL and DICK, the property of the subscribers.—Gill is a dark mulatto, with short wooly hair; is about five feet six inches high; stout made; has square shoulders, bow legs, and walks clumsily.—Had on when he went away a homespun coat, and vest a mixture of black and white, half lapelled; trowsers **twilled** homespun, a smutty brown, and considerably worn—he also took with him two striped vests, and sundry other articles of clothing.

twilled: A weave of fabric that has a surface of diagonal parallel ridges.

DICK is a short thick set fellow, about 5 feet 4 inches high; remarkably black; has a scar on his cheek and another on his chin.—He had on and took with him a variety of cloathing—among other articles, a short coat without skirts; the color a mixture of blue with hemlock; nankeen overhails &c.

Whoever will apprehend and secure the said Runaways so that they may be had, shall be entitled to the above reward, or Three Guineas for either of them separately.
REUBEN WILLIAMS
JAMES PETERS
Gagetown, August [12?], 1799.

41 *Royal Gazette*, 20 August 1799.

DOCUMENT 36:
Female Sold for a Term of Years, Nova Scotia, 1800[42]

In this document, Michael Houseal hoped to sell his black servant for a set number of years. It was common for slave-owners in the United States to hire out their slaves to less wealthy white neighbours who could not afford to purchase a slave. In this case, the young woman might have been enslaved or an indentured servant from whom the owner wanted to make a profit since we know from the rest of the advertisement that he intended to go to England.

ALSO,
For Sale for a Term of Years, as may be agreed on, a likely stout, NEGRO GIRL, Aged 18 years, good natured, fond of children and accustomed to both Town and Country work.—For particulars enquire at the old Parsonage, Dutch Town.

---

42 *Royal Gazette*, 24 June 1800.

DOCUMENT 37:

Runaway Slave Advertisement, Two Slaves, New Brunswick, 1802[43]

It was somewhat unusual for slaves to run away in the Maritimes during the height of winter. In this case, two enslaved light-skinned men absconded together, likely to escape the harsh treatment of their owner. The poem appeared directly below the runaway slave advertisement. I have not seen another one like it; perhaps it is a commentary on slaveholding.

FONTABELLE, *Westmoreland*, 14th 1802.
ABSCONDED the middle of December last, two able young Negro men belonging to the Subscriber—one named *Trim* and the other *Jimmey*, supposed a Nayo, marked A.R. on the left shoulder, and had a sore on one of his feet near the ancle; both rather of a yellow complexion, and middle sized. Whoever will lodge either of the above negroes in any gaol or work-house in this Island, will be entitled to a Reward of *Five Pounds* for each, or shall prove to conviction any person harbouring or concealing either of them, to a Reward of *Twenty pounds*, from [name not given].

Since God precedes to ease this way,
Join in chorus and say—
Man or Christian what am I,
That to Africa deny?
With tenderness as fed with care, and when
He trips the paves so light,
His head adorn'd, his heart is light;
He is by every learned man to find his way
And to maintain his right,
And not possess'd of human light
Born in ignorance, and live in sin,
Concealing cruel laws within;
They who have that chain to patch,
With perseverance Match't,
It's there and ready at your call,
And if it's broke you are rob'd of all.
Thomas P——.

---

43 *Royal Gazette*, 15 December 1802.

DOCUMENT 38:
Runaway Slave Advertisement, Dinah, New Brunswick, 1806[44]

In the Maritimes, black women sometimes encountered predatory and potentially sexually abusive—if not obsessive—owners seemingly willing to go further in trying to prevent escapes of slave women. An example of this is John Ryan's shocking advertisement in New Brunswick's *Royal Gazette*. Ryan's stark warning to any anti-slavery individuals and his preemptory slave advertisement for a woman before she had actually attempted to escape is remarkable. What was actually going on between Dinah and Ryan? Why did Ryan think he needed to exercise so much control over this female slave? The advertisement strongly suggests personal issues and an abusive relationship (beyond the typical abuse inherent in the master/slave encounter) between Ryan and Dinah. This advertisement is unique, and I have not come across something similar for a male slave.

CAUTION.

THE Subscriber hereby cautions all persons against attempting in future to seduce from his Service his Female Negro Slave DINAH, (for whom he has a good legal title)—as he is determined to punish by all legal ways and means, every offender of that description.—And that no one may plead ignorance of the person of the Slave in excuse, he informs all concerned, that she is about 26 years of age—4 feet 9 inches high—has a small scar upon her forehead—and lately belonged to Mr. JAMES TAYLOR, of Maugerville.

JOHN RYAN.

Saint John, 19th, Nov. 1806.

44 *Royal Gazette*, 24 December 1806.

DOCUMENT 39:
Slave for Sale, Nancy, New Brunswick, 1809[45]

In this short document, a slaveholder offers a black woman for sale. The interesting aspect about this for sale notice is that the Nancy listed below might be the same one who tried to escape from Caleb Jones with Lidge and several others in 1786 (see Document 19, p. 47). She might also be the woman who was the centrepiece of New Brunswick's famous 1800 slave court case that returned a woman named Nancy to slavery (see Document 62, p. 114).

FOR SALE
A NEGRO WENCH, named NANCY, belonging to the Subscriber.—a good title will be given.
October 6, 1809. D. BROWN.

45 *Royal Gazette*, 16 October 1809.

DOCUMENT 40:

Runaway Slave Advertisement, Lidge Escapes Again, New Brunswick, 1816[46]

Lidge still wanted his freedom despite 30 years of enslavement after his original escape attempt at the age of four with Nancy and other slaves (see Document 19, p. 47). Since Caleb Jones died without a will six months after placing this advertisement. Lidge's fate is unclear, but slavery in New Brunswick, while still existing in the late 1810s, was slowly dying out and being replaced with various forms of servitude or wage labour.

Twelve Dollars Reward

RUN AWAY from the Subscriber,

On the night of the 15th June, a Negro Slave, called LIDGE, under five feet high, broad face and very large lips; brought him from Maryland with my family;—he took with him a large CANOE with a Lathe across her; tared on the outside of the head with raw Tar, which looks red—he was seen going down the River[.] Any person that will apprehend him and get the canoe, shall receive the above reward.

CALEB JONES,

9th July 1816.

---

46 *Royal Gazette*, 9 July 1816.

DOCUMENT 41:

Runaway Advertisement, Samuel Hutchings, New Brunswick, 1818[47]

This was one of the last runaway notices in the Maritimes. It is not clear if Hutchings was enslaved or an indentured servant. He was certainly unfree.

RUNAWAY
ON Wednesday evening last, from the Subscriber, a Negro Boy, named Samuel Hutchings.—All persons are forbid harbouring or trusting him on my account.
JOHN MOUNT.
Musquash, 4th September 1818.

47 *New Brunswick Courier*, 5 September 1818.

PART II

Letters, Narratives, Newspapers, Petitions

In this part, readers will have the opportunity to explore documents which offer personal views and experiences with slavery in the Maritimes. Specifically, a few of these documents were written (or dictated) by slaves or former slaves. It is very rare for historians to glean unmediated black voices from the available documentary evidence. The petitions offer a view into how enslaved people and formerly enslaved people understood their own lives. These documents also include the words of slave-owners and how they viewed their slaves and their own role as masters.

DOCUMENT 42:

John Wentworth Letter about His 19 Slaves, Nova Scotia, 1784[1]

In this document, John Wentworth, the former Royal Governor of New Hampshire shipped 19 slaves to his relative in Surinam (South America). He kept at least two slaves at his home in Nova Scotia. This is the largest documented shipment of slaves from Nova Scotia to the Caribbean or South America. Readers should pay close attention to the work patterns and names of the slaves. Clearly, these slaves had a wide variety of occupational backgrounds. Wentworth's words of affection for his slaves did not prevent him from sending them to a much more brutal form of slavery.

Halifax, Nova Scotia, Feb. 24 1784

Sir,

I herewith Inclose to you a Bill of Lading for 19 Negro Slaves, shipped by me on board [schooner] *Polly*, Samuel Little Master. For account and to be Employed on the Estates and for the use of my dearest friend [and] relation Paul Wentworth, Esq. I also herewith Inclose a Receipt for sundry Provisions shipped for the Use of these Slaves, And it is agreed that the Surplus of their Consumption shall be delivered to you free of all Expences [order?] and whatsoever. This Addition of valuable Slaves I trust will be exceedingly useful as they are all either American born or well seasoned, and are perfectly stout, healthy, sober, orderly, Industrious, & obedient. Isaac, is a [thorough] good Carpenter & Master Sawyer perfectly capable of overseeing & conducting the rest and strictly honest. Lymas, is a rough carpenter & Sawyer; Quako is a field Negro, has met an Accident in his arm, which will require some Indulgence. The other men are Sawyers and John also a good axe man. Abraham has been used to Cattle and to Attend in the House, etc. All the men are expert in boats. The women, are stout, able, & promise well to increase their numbers. Venus, is useful in ye Hospital, Poultry yards, Gardens. Upon the whole they are a most useful lot of Negroes and have behaved so intirely well and to my Approbation that I earnestly recommend them to your particular care. And if practicable that they be employed together and that Isaac should be their overseer. I am much

1 John Wentworth to Paul Wentworth or his attorney, 24 February 1784, Wentworth Letters, vol. 49, NSA.

interested for them, insomuch that I had them christened, and would rather have liberated them, then sent them to my Estate that I was not assured of their being treated with care and humanity, which I shall consider as the only favor that can be done to me on this Occasion ... About three months since I wrote to Mr. W to London That I had purchased these Negroes, and should ship them in March for his Estate at Surinam....

J. Wentworth
Negroes Embarked

Abraham	Priscilla
James	Rachel
Henry	Venus
Lymas	Daphne
Cyrus	Ann
John	
Isaac	6 Dorothy
Quako	
9 January	
	Children
	Celia
	William
	Venus
	4 Elenora

Matthew
Susannah } reserved at Home
The above all Christened by Dr. Breynton Feb. 11, 1784

DOCUMENT 43:

Petition of Zimri Armstrong about Re-enslavement, New Brunswick, 1785[2]

Local records are replete with sad examples of husbands and wives or parents and children being separated by the whims of an owner. In 1785, Zimri Armstrong petitioned the Governor of New Brunswick. Armstrong had "agread [sic]" to work for Samuel Jarvis for two years as long as Jarvis paid for his passage to New Brunswick and purchased the freedom of Armstrong's family, who were slaves. During Armstrong's indenture, Samuel Jarvis had transferred control of Armstrong to his brother and returned to the United States. According to Armstrong, Samuel Jarvis "left me destitute of both Cloaths and provisions in a Strange Country ... [and] had sold my wife and family." Armstrong then petitioned the provincial government, stating that he should be freed from his service. Governor Thomas Carleton, however, showed scant concern for the slave or free black population in New Brunswick, and the provincial council had little interest in helping Armstrong. The only option for Armstrong was to pursue his complaint through the court system, which he lacked the resources to do. In this instance, Armstrong lost his family and his own freedom for a period of years.

Please note this document required some editing to be readable.

To His Excellency Thos. Carlton Govr. Capt. Genl. And Commdr. in Chief in and over the Province of New Brunswick and the Territories There on Depending Chancellor and Vice Adml. of the Same &c &c &c

The Humble Memorial of Zimri Armstrong most Humbly Sheweth that Having agreed with Saml. Jarvis in Stanford in Connecticut[3] in New England that the aforesaid Saml. Jarvis for and in the consideration of my serving him for the space of two years did bind himself to me that he would purchase my wife and family and pay my passage hear to this province and after my being free was to set me up at my trade when I Came to this province the aforesaid Saml. Jarvis sold his land and went back to the States having left me destitute of both Cloaths and provisions in a strange Country to provide for myself after my being sick. Neither Saml. Jarvis nor either of his brothers gave me the value of one penny to support me when I was not able to support myself and now is gone back and sold my wife

2 Zimri Armstrong, Saint John's County, no. 78, F 1024, RS 108, Land Petitions, PANB.

3 The author means Stamford, Connecticut.

and family. Now John Jarvis demands me as his in behalf of his brother to serve out my time which is almost expired. Turn over.

I went to [**Mr. Leonard**] esquire to demand my provisions of the aforesaid Jno. Jarvis when his worship was pleased to send a warrant for him and when he came there he told [Mr. Leonard] that his brother Saml. Jarvis was to be here within the space of six weeks of which he was willing to take his oath before [Mr. Leonard] when I contented myself for a while when I was at last Credibly informed that Saml. Jarvis had sold my wife and family when I again went to [Mr. Leonard] and he then owned before [Mr. Leonard] that his brother had sold them I never got my provisions or any [likelihood] of my getting Clearance of him. He have stop my provisions till I went to Mr. Knox who gave me an order for to draw it before I went to Mr. Knox he sent to the Captain of the Comp. That I did belong to draw my provision for himself but Capt. Whitmore refused to give it to him till he got an order I have drawn some [flour] and the meat I can get when I go to Capt. Whitmore. Since I came here I have drawn neither land or Cloaths being almost naked for them all to that Saml. Jarvis according to agreement never gave me any nor his brother Jno. Jarvis who now keeps me if your excellency will grant [me my] petition that is to let me know weather he can keep me or know if not as I can produce the paper about our agreement between me and Saml. Jarvis and as I can bring proof of what is here inserted [by credible] people in this town and if there is any land to spare to grant me some as well as other indigent loyalists I shall be duty bound and ever pray for your excellency health and prosperity.

Mr. Leonard: Probably George Leonard. Originally from Massachusetts, he opposed the American Revolution from the earliest disturbances in Boston and fought at Lexington. After migrating to Saint John, he served as director of the town, eventually an alderman, and finally became a member of council in 1790. See Ann Gorman Condon, "Leonard, George," in *Dictionary of Canadian Biography*, vol. 6, University of Toronto/Université Laval.

your most humble memorialist
Zimri Armstrong

DOCUMENT 44:

James MacGregor, A Letter to a *Clergyman Urging him to set free a Black Girl he held in SLAVERY*, Nova Scotia, 1788[4]

James MacGregor wrote an important early anti-slavery pamphlet attacking a local clergyman for enslaving his fellow human beings. This letter was directed at the Reverend Daniel Cock, who had owned and sold female slaves. MacGregor saw no excuse for slaveholding and accordingly argued that Cock, who had obtained a slave woman as a gift and had purchased her daughter, was "under the necessity of renouncing every thing amiable, divine or humane, before the curse of Canaan entitle you to enslave your fellow creatures." This document is full of various refutations of slavery and the slave trade. I encourage readers to look up the entire letter on their own.

You plead that it is better for them to be slaves than to be free. Is it then in the height of your generosity that you enslave? It is because you love your neighbor so dearly as to prefer his welfare to your own? Give me leave to suspect this excessive generosity. I am afraid that among the slave-traders, there are some sordid wretches that would not suffer the Negroes to continue in slavery if that were best; but they would strive to get the best state for themselves, and yet I see no emulation among them to exchange with their slaves. Besides, it is not easy to conceive how beats and [?], blood and wounds, bruises and broken bones are desirable things, or preferable to a safe and whole skin. But you will say, though slavery be not beneficial to all yet it is so to the Negroes, for they are different from all people, and have a disposition peculiar to themselves, and experience shews that they thrive better bound than free. I would ask, is it their great Master in Heaven that hath given them that slavish disposition, which turns liberty into a curse?

4 James MacGregor, A Letter to a *Clergyman Urging him to set free a Black Girl he held in SLAVERY* (Halifax: A Henry, 1788), 8.

DOCUMENT 45:

Petition of Thomas Peters to the British Government, 1790[5]

In 1790, the Black Loyalist Thomas Peters sent two petitions to the British Secretary of State for Foreign Affairs describing the difficulties people of African descent faced in the Maritime colonies. Originally from Africa and having served in the British armed forces during the Revolutionary War, Peters became an outspoken critic of broken British promises to the Black Loyalist community. Peters eventually became one of the leading advocates for black resettlement in Sierra Leone. His petition highlights the role of slavery, re-enslavement, and racism in Nova Scotia and New Brunswick. Readers should note Peters' emphasis on the new rights that black people should have as free subjects of King George III. Peters and others were claiming protection and rights that they felt free black inhabitants of British colonies deserved. At the same time, Peters criticized Nova Scotia for its treatment of free blacks and slaves.

To the Rt. Hon. Lord Grenville one of His Majesty's principal Secretaries of State.

The humble Petition of Thomas Peters, a Negro, late Serjeant in the Regiment of Guides & Pioneers serving in North America in the late War under the Command of **Gen. Sir Henry Clinton**, and now deputed by his Fellow Soldiers and by other Free Negroes and People of Colour Refugees, settled at Annapolis, Digby and St. John's [New Brunswick] in Nova Scotia

Gen. Sir Henry Clinton: Commander in Chief of the British Forces from 1778 to 1782. In 1779, he issued a proclamation that promised protection for any slave who deserted a rebel owner and came to British lines.

Humbly sheweth

That the Situation of your Memorialist and of the other free Negroes and People of Colour above mentioned is rendered extremely irksome and disadvantageous not only by the Want of the promised Allotments of Land which they cannot yet obtain (as represented in another memorial) though seven Years are elapsed since their Arrival in the Province appointed for their Settlement, but more especially they are injured also by a public and avowed Toleration of Slavery in Nova Scotia as if the happy Influence of his Majesty's free Government was incapable of being extended so far as

5 Thomas Peters to Lord Grenville, "The Humble Petition of Thomas Peters, A Negro," 1790, FO 4/1, C 308757, the National Archives, London, UK.

America to "maintain Justice and Right" in affording the Protection of the Laws & Constitution of England.

That even the King's Courts in Nova Scotia have publicly decided in Favour of Slavery, and refused the Protection of the Laws to the poor Negroes in that unhappy state which has occasioned such a degrading and unjust Prejudice against People of Colour in general that even those that are acknowledged to be free Inhabitants and Settlers in the Province are refused the common Rights and Privileges of the other Inhabitants, not being permitted to vote at any Election nor to serve on Juries whereby it is become very difficult for them to obtain ordinary Justice in the Recovery of Debts due to them for Labour or even to obtain common Protection from Violence and personal Ill Usage, insomuch that several of them [through] this notorious Partiality or "Respect of Persons" (which is absolutely forbid and even deemed odious in the Laws of England) have already been reduced to Slavery without being able to obtain any Redress from the King's Courts, And that one of them thus reduced to Slavery did actually lose his Life by the Beating and Ill Treatment of his Master and another who fled from the like Cruelty was inhumanely shot and maimed by a Stranger allured thereto by the public advertisement of a Reward for such unnatural Violence who "delivered him up to his Master" in that deplorable wounded State. [A]ltho' the Laws of God (and of Course also the Common Law of England) have absolutely prohibited "[delivering] up to his Master the Servant" (or Slave) "that has escaped from his Master" (Deut. 23.15). And as the poor friendless Slaves have no more Protection by the Laws of the Colony (as they are at present misunderstood) than the mere [**chattel**] or brute Beasts, their Treatment ... is also similar or even worse than the Treatment of Cattle, as the Caprice & Passions of wicked Men are more liable to be excited against human Beings than against dumb Animals; and that the oppressive Cruelty and Brutality of their Bondage is in General shocking to human Nature but more particularly shocking—irritating and obnoxious to their Brethren of the same Kindred the free People of Colour who cannot conceive that it is really the Intention of the British Government to favour Injustice, or tolerate Slavery in Nova Scotia where the Nature of the Climate does not afford even the false Pretence of Necessity for Evil (so frequently alleged for the Evil of Slavery in the West Indies) as it is less congenial to Blacks than Whites, and therefore they humbly and earnestly implore Protection and Redress.

chattel: Personal property.

Thomas Peters His Mark

DOCUMENT 46:
John Clarkson's Diary, Lydia Jackson's Re-enslavement and Other Observations, 1791[6]

John Clarkson served as an officer in the British Royal Navy. The brother of the famous anti-slavery activist Thomas Clarkson, John helped organize the exodus of some Black Loyalists from Nova Scotia to Sierra Leone. During his time in Nova Scotia, Clarkson kept a very detailed diary of his experiences with enslaved black people, free Black Loyalists, and the local white population. Some of the most poignant and telling stories about black people in Nova Scotia come from his diary, especially the case of Lydia Jackson.

28th October. Employed as yesterday. Upon inquiry I found that the greatest part of the people who had given in their names had not done it with the idea of improving their own condition, but for the sake of their children whom they wish to see established (as they expressed it) upon a better foundation—

A most affecting scene occurred this afternoon occasioned by a Black *slave* who came to me in order to resign his wife and family who were free.

With tears streaming down his cheeks he said, that though this separation would be as death to himself, yet he had come to a resolution of resigning them up for ever, convinced as he was, that such a measure would ultimately tend to render their situation more comfortable and happy—He said he was regardless of himself or of the cruelties he might hereafter experience for though sunk to the most [abject] state of wretchedness he could at all times cheer himself with the pleasing reflection that his wife and children were happy—

Much more he said, which is impossible to convey in language adequate to our feelings on this occasion....

November 30th—Waited upon Mr. Bulkeley the President of Council who received me with attention and promised to do everything in his power to forward my business and further said that & every other gentleman would and ought to do every thing in their power to assist me, who had upon every occasion conducted myself with so much candour & fairness—Came home, received several visits from people of every description and of whom was a young woman a Black named Lydia Jackson; her case which I have taken

6 C.B. Fergusson, ed., *Clarkson's Mission to America, 1791–1792* (Halifax: Public Archives of Nova Scotia, 1971), 56–57, 89–90.

from her own mouth I shall relate since it will serve to give some idea of the situation of the Black people in this Province.

Mr. Henry Hedley of Manchester finding Lydia Jackson in great distress having been left by her husband, he invited her to come & reside in his house, to live as a companion to his wife, after she had been there for seven days, he required her either to pay him for her board and bind herself to him for seven years; she was unable to pay him and refused to be bound; at length gradually shortening the period by a year at a time, he by dint of fair promises obtained her consent to be indented to him for one year; the writings were in consequence drawn up by a Mr. Harrison of the same place, but taking advantage of her ignorance the term of thirty nine years was specified in the Indenture, instead of the one she had consented to; and to this paper she without the least suspicion made her mark—Henry Hedley told her the next day that she was to serve out the year with Dr. Bulman of Lunenburg and sent her round for this purpose in a Schooner commanded by Alexander Brymer, Dr. Bulman soon after her arrival at Lunenburg informed her to her great astonishment that she had been articled for the term of thirty nine years, and that she had been made over to him for the consideration of £20 which he had paid to Henry Hedley.

Dr. Bulman turned out to be a very bad master, frequently beating her with the tongs, sticks, pieces of rope &c. about the head & face, his wife likewise was by no means backward to lend him her assistance on these occasions. For some words she had spoken with the least intention of giving offence Bulman took occasion to knock her down, and though she was then in the last month of pregnancy, in the most inhuman manner, stamped upon her whilst she lay upon the ground; for these and other cruelties she lodged a complaint against him before Mr. Lambert an Attorney at Lunenburg. This gentleman took up her case which was brought into Court but was soon silenced by the overbearing manners & influence of Bulman, who then or soon after expressed his intention of selling her to some Planter in the West Indies to work as a slave. In the meantime he sent her to work upon his farm about three miles from the town, giving authority and sanction to his servants to beat & punish her as they thought fit. After she had continued with Dr. Bulman three years, she made her escape in a wonderful way through the woods & after experiencing innumerable hardships, she reached Halifax, and got a Memorial drawn up and Presented to the Governor, who paid little or no attention to it. At length she applied to the Chief Justice, who promised to enquire into the business and lastly she came to me. I immediately wrote to Dr. Bulman respecting her and consulted a Lawyer on the business who gave it as his opinion that her wages could be recovered for the time she lived under Bulman but the forms of law would most likely prevent its being finally settled, so as to enable her to go with me. Finding there was no chance of the business being settled, while I remained in the Province I advised her to give it up and leave Bulman to his own reflections.

I do not know what induced me to mention the above story, as I have many others of a similar nature; for example, Scott's case, Mr. Lee, Senr. Case, Smith's child, Motly Roads child, Mr. Farish's negro servant, &c.

DOCUMENT 47:

Thomas Clarkson, "Some Account of the New Colony at Sierra Leone," Re-enslavement, 1792[7]

Lord Dunmore ... General Clinton: In November 1775, the Royal Governor of Virginia, Lord Dunmore, issued a proclamation offering freedom to slaves of Patriot owners in an attempt to stem the rising tide of war. Thousands of slaves escaped to British lines and attempted to claim their freedom. Later in the war, Sir Henry Clinton issued another proclamation offering slaves of Patriot owners freedom and future protection.

In this article, British anti-slavery activist Thomas Clarkson, the brother of John Clarkson, described the process of black re-enslavement in the Maritimes. He discusses how black people fought for the British as a result of several military proclamations (beginning with **Lord Dunmore's 1775 proclamation and followed by General Clinton**), which offered freedom to slaves who escaped from Patriot owners, not their Loyalist slave-owning counterparts, and aided His Majesty's war effort. These men and women were promised not only freedom, but land and decent treatment as new subjects of the British Empire. Clarkson's harsh view of white American Loyalists emanates from his revulsion at their treatment of black people who had fought alongside white Loyalists and attempted to help them win the Revolutionary War. Clarkson's brother and possibly the Black Loyalist Thomas Peters were probably the sources of information for the article.

DURING the American war, among other modes of raising soldiers adopted by the British generals, a proclamation had been made by General Clinton, that every negro slave, who should join the British forces, should obtain his freedom, and have a settlement at the conclusion of the war. Many accordingly came in, were enrolled in the army, and, on the peace, had tickets of freedom given them by the officers under whom they had served. Lands were allotted them in Nova Scotia, where, with many other loyalists, they were sent by government, when hostilities were at an end. It was not long till these loyalists, many of whom had been educated with all the ideas of the justice of slavery, the inferiority of negroes, and the superiority of white men, that are universal in the southern provinces of America, began to harass and oppress the industrious black settlers and even wantonly to deprive them of the fruits of their labor, expelling them from the lands they had cleared, and, without any compensation, appropriating these to their own use. The courts of law, composed of white men, connected with the oppressors, gave no redress ... [White Loyalists and British officers] made frequent and successful attempts to reduce again to slavery those negroes who had so honourably obtained their freedom. They hired them as servants, and, at the

7 Thomas Clarkson, "Some Account of the New Colony at Sierra Leone," *The American Museum; or Universal Magazine*, May 1792.

end of the stipulated time, refused payment of their wages, insisting that they were slaves; in some instances they destroyed their tickets of freedom, and then enslaved the negroes for want of them.

DOCUMENT 48:
David George's Narrative, 1793[8]

Born in Virginia, David George had a series of owners including Aboriginal slaveholders. Eventually, he ended up in Silver Bluff, South Carolina and became one of the founding members of the African American Baptist church. During the American Revolution, he gained his freedom and migrated to Nova Scotia. Here, he encountered severe racism and discrimination as illustrated by the 1784 race riot in Shelburne. George devoted his time in Nova Scotia to spreading the Christian Gospel and baptizing people. In 1792, he left Nova Scotia and settled in Sierra Leone. His account gives readers an opportunity to understand post-revolutionary Nova Scotia from the perspective of a former American slave who had meaningful contact with those who were still enslaved in the Maritimes. In this excerpt, he discusses baptizing several servants (probably enslaved or indentured) and racism.

... When I was landing at St. John's [Saint John, New Brunswick], some of the people who intended to be baptized were so full of joy that they ran out from waiting at table on their masters, with knives and forks in their hands, to meet me at the water side. This second time of my being at St. John's I staid preaching about a fortnight, and baptized ten people. Our going down into the water seemed to be a pleasing sight to the whole town, White people and Black.

Clarkson: John Clarkson helped lead the exodus of Black Loyalists from the Maritimes to Sierra Leone. He kept a detailed diary of his experiences in Nova Scotia and New Brunswick, which is one of the best primary sources historians have for race relations in the late-eighteenth-century Maritimes. He later became governor of the British colony in Sierra Leone. (See Document 46, p. 81)

... The next fall, Agent (afterwards Governor) **Clarkson** came to Halifax, about settling the new colony of Sierra Leone. The White people in Nova Scotia were very unwilling that we should go,[9] though they had been very cruel to us and treated many of us as bad as though we had been slaves.

---

8 David George, "An Account of the Life of Mr. DAVID GEORGE, from Sierra Leone in Africa; given by himself in a Conversation with Brother RIPPON of London, and Brother [Samuel] PEARCE [1766–99] of Birmingham" *BAPTIST ANNUAL REGISTER, FOR 1790, 1791, 1792, AND PART OF 1793*, cited in Vincent Carretta, ed., *Unchained Voices: An Anthology of Black Authors in the English-Speaking World of the 18th Century* (1996, expanded edition, Lexington: UP of Kentucky, 2004), 333–50.

9 This was because the free blacks represented a source of cheap labour.

DOCUMENT 49:
Boston King's Narrative, 1798[10]

Born in South Carolina, Boston King escaped to British lines during the American Revolution and gained his freedom. A skilled carpenter, he was unable to find gainful employment in Nova Scotia and ended up doing manual day-to-day labouring work. He became a Methodist preacher and eventually migrated to Sierra Leone. The following excerpt highlights King's deeply held Christian beliefs and the struggles he went through to become free. Please note that the British brought thousands of former and still enslaved black people (and many white Loyalists) to New York City and evacuated them in 1783.

Sometimes I thought, if it was the will of GOD that I should be a slave, I was ready to resign myself to his will; but at other times I could not find the least desire to content myself in slavery. When I arrived at New-York, my friends rejoiced to see me once more restored to liberty, and joined me in praising the Lord for his mercy and goodness....

... About which time, (in 1783), the horrors and devastation of war happily terminated, and peace was restored between America and Great Britain which diffused the universal joy among all parties, except us, who had escaped from slavery, and taken refuge in the English army; for a report prevailed at New-York, that all slaves, in number 2,000,[11] were to be delivered up to their masters, altho' some of them had been three or four years among the English. This dreadful rumour filled us all with inexpressible anguish and terror, especially when we saw our old masters coming from Virginia, North-Carolina, and other parts, and seizing upon their slaves in the streets of New-York, or even dragging them out of their beds. Many of the slaves had very cruel masters so that the thoughts of returning home with them embittered life to us. For some days we lost our appetite for food, and sleep departed from our eyes. The English had compassion upon us in the day of distress and issued out a proclamation importing, That all slaves should be free,[12] who had taken refuge in the British lines, and claimed the sanction

---

10 Boston King, "Memoirs of the Life of BOSTON KING, a Black Preacher. Written by Himself, during his Residence at Kingswoods-School," *The Methodist Magazine for MARCH 1798* (London, 1798), cited in Carretta, ed., *Unchained Voices*, 351–68.

11 The actual number was greater than this.

12 Meaning those who ran away to British lines from their rebel owners, not those enslaved to Loyalists or British army officers.

and privileges of the proclamations respecting the security and protection of Negroes.[13] In consequence of this, each of us received a certificate from the commanding officer at New-York,[14] which dispelled all our fears, and filled us with joy and gratitude. Soon after, ships were fitted out, and furnished with every necessary for conveying us to Nova Scotia.

13 See Lord Dunmore and Sir Henry Clinton's respective proclamations.

14 He is referring to their General Birch Certificates.

DOCUMENT 50:

Gradual Emancipation of Jack and Amelia in Prince Edward Island, 1800[15]

In this document, Prince Edward Island slave-owner Colonel Joseph Robinson offers conditional freedom to his two slaves. These slaves, Jack and Amelia, had a few children who Robinson also owned. Readers should carefully read this excerpt from the memorandum book. Although Robinson owned Jack and Amelia, it is clear that his slaves also had agency in gaining their freedom. Slavery was complicated and it is far too simple to assume that slaves had no cards they could play. For example, there are various types of negotiation coexisting in Robinson's note. The first sentence of his entry is profoundly revealing. Robinson wrote that he was "under the necessity" of telling his slaves about their impending move to Prince Town. Let us ask why he felt compelled to tell them anything. They were his slaves after all. Yet the first sentence demonstrates that Robinson felt like he could not just tell his slaves what to do. Robinson did not simply make Amelia and Jack leave their home, but rather he explained to them—that is, he negotiated with the two slaves—why they should go to Prince Town. Indeed, Robinson had to sweeten the deal or face two discontented or resistant slaves.

He thus offered freedom to the couple, while simultaneously denying it to their children, but this gave the slaves a chance to seize their own freedom. As the historian Ira Berlin argues, slaves could negotiate their freedom, but it was a tricky business. Robinson had most of the advantages, including an understanding of the law and more material resources than his slaves. His notation left little doubt as to his goal of controlling his slaves' behaviour by placing demeaning demands on them. Indeed, like many slaveholders who offered conditional **manumission** throughout North America, Robinson could not, "resist squeezing [his] slaves one last time."[16] But Jack and Amelia were far from helpless. They could call upon a reservoir of knowledge about their owners and "the support of family and community."[17] The tenor of Robinson's note reveals a man trying to convince himself that he still controlled his slaves by attempting to put various types of restrictions on Jack and Amelia's potential liberty. Yet his slaves did in some ways control their path to freedom if "they behaved themselves." They knew how to please Robinson and his wife after years of service to them. The enslaved couple could use this knowledge to obtain freedom. However, the continued

manumission: When a slave-owner freed a slave.

15 *Examiner*, 11 February 1881 (the original memorandum book has not survived).

16 Ira Berlin, *Many Thousands Gone: The First Two Centuries of Slavery in North America* (Cambridge, MA: Harvard UP, 1998), 235.

17 Berlin, *Thousands*, 235.

enslavement of their children presented financial challenges that required the couple to slowly build up enough money to purchase their children's liberty. Jack and Amelia's opportunity for freedom is an example of the negotiations that took place between slaveholders and slaves throughout the Atlantic world including the Maritime colonies. These two slaves did not have the best cards to play, but they did have some cards and could win a hand against their owners, which might result in freedom or the amelioration of certain conditions.

19th July 1800—I was under the necessity of telling my servants, Jack and Amelia to get them to go to Prince Town—that at the end of one year, if they behaved themselves well (of which I was to be the judge) and that neither Mrs. ——— or myself wanted either of them, I would give them their liberty; that is to say, only for themselves two, not liberty for any children they now have or may hereafter have. But I also told them that if they or either of them misbehaved, they forfeit all expectations thereto. I also told them as long as either of us wanted them, they were not to look for or expect their liberty, but to remain slaves as long as we or either of us, thought proper.

DOCUMENT 51:

Joseph Aplin's Racial Justification for Slavery, 1801[18]

Joseph Aplin served as an attorney for slaveholders in the late eighteenth and early nineteenth centuries. He would eventually serve as the attorney general of Prince Edward Island. In this document, he bluntly describes black people as naturally fit for slavery.

Why are they black and we white, there can be nothing more diametrically opposite to each other than those two colours, which serves to evince their inferiority to us. [I]t may be said that their colour is owing to the Climate in which they reside. If it was why are not those who live under the same parallels of Latitude, of the like cast? No doubt can remain that they were designed to be subservient to others: therefore [black people] may be very justly termed slaves by Nature.

18 Joseph Aplin to Sampson Salter Blowers, Opinion Supporting Lawfulness of Slavery, 1801, F51 Correspondence, etc., 1785–1822, Odell Family Collections, S29B-F51, NBM.

DOCUMENT 52:

Excerpts from *Opinions of Several Gentlemen of the Law, on the Subject of Negro Servitude in the Province of Nova-Scotia*, 1802[19]

The authors of this pamphlet, especially Loyalist Joseph Aplin, wished to show that slavery was legal in Nova Scotia through an examination of James DeLancey's case to recover his slave named Jack (see Document 61, p. 112). A pro-slavery attorney with racist views (see previous document), Aplin argued that the British Parliament had sanctioned slavery and the slave trade throughout its colonial dominions ranging from Jamaica to Virginia to Nova Scotia. It should be noted that the best legal minds in Nova Scotia, including the Chief Justice S.S. Blowers, strongly disagreed with Aplin's views.

Hence we may safely argue, that as several acts of the British Parliament do make Slaves of Negroes; and as all His Majesty's Subjects [whether British or Colonial] are made equal sharers in the profits of the African or Negro traffic, The Colonial Traders might carry their Slaves, either to the West-Indies, or to any other of His Majesty's Colonies on the Continent. Consequently, if Negroes so imported into the West-Indies, were legally held as slaves there, they cannot, when imported into any of the Continental Colonies, be in a better state than they would have been, had they been imported into the West-Indies.

19 *Opinions of Several Gentlemen of the Law, on the Subject of Negro Servitude in the Province of Nova-Scotia* (St. John: John Ryan, 1802), 10.

DOCUMENT 53:
Digby Slave-Owners' Petition, Nova Scotia, 1807[20]

The Digby petition is one of the most important documents about Maritime slavery. It gives detailed information about the number of male, female, and child slaves within various households. It is the only document that so clearly lays out slaveholding households with a clear breakdown of enslaved persons. Readers should examine the petitioners' clear discomfort with slavery, but also note their determination to receive compensation if their slaves gained freedom. The petition also illuminates the frustration of slaveholders, who, complained that their slaves were becoming increasingly disobedient and defiant.

3 December 1807

To the Honorable the Representatives for His Majestys Province of Nova Scotia in General Assembly convened,
The Petition of the Subscribers, proprietors of Negro Servants, brought from His Majestys late Colonies now called the United States of America

Most humbly sheweth,

That, prior to the late American Revolution, your petitioners were inhabitants of His Majestys late revolted Colonies;

That, when His Majestys authority began to be opposed in those Colonies, your petitioners adhered to their allegiance, and [received] the Royal assurance of full protection to their persons and security to their properties;

That, at that period, throughout all of His Majestys Colonies (without any exception) a property in Negroes was maintained and acknowledged if not encouraged; And your petitioners know not of any public act since that time, whereby such sort of property has been declared untenable—On the contrary, the Royal Proclamations and the Acts of Parliament admitting and encouraging persons of your petitioners political principles to remove out of the United States into this Province, expressly authorise them to bring their Negro Slaves,—

Your petitioners are far from pretending to advocate Slavery as a System. With the creation of that System they had nothing to do. The introduction of Negro Slaves into His Majestys Colonies was at a time long before your

20 Petition of John Taylor and Others, Negro Proprietors, to the General Assembly, December 1807, RG 5 A, Box 14, doc. 49, NSA.

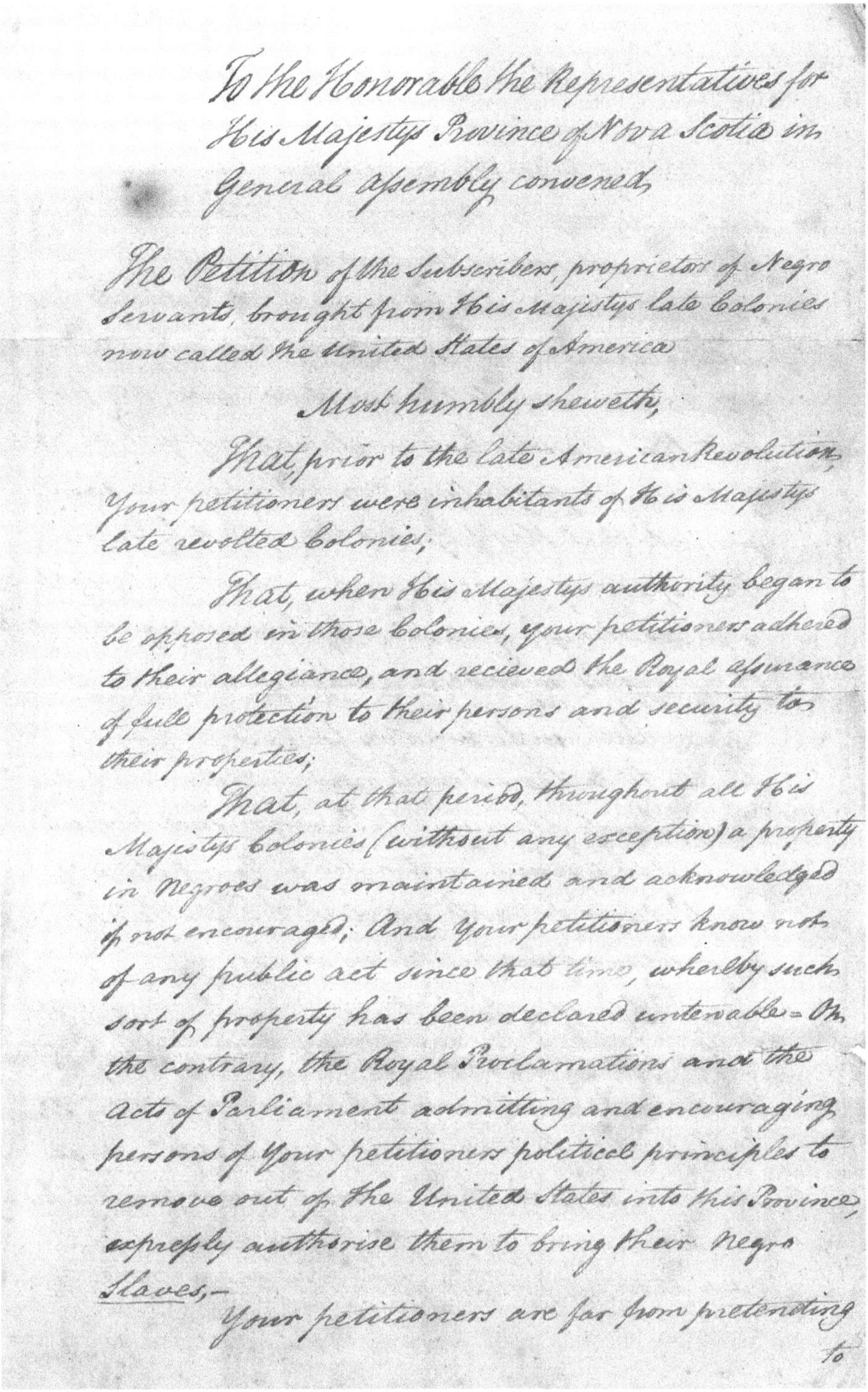

To the Honorable the Representatives for
His Majestys Province of Nova Scotia in
General assembly convened,

The Petition of the Subscribers, proprietors of Negro
Servants, brought from His Majestys late Colonies
now called the United States of America

Most humbly sheweth,

That, prior to the late American Revolution,
Your petitioners were inhabitants of His Majestys
late revolted Colonies;

That, when His Majestys authority began to
be opposed in those Colonies, your petitioners adhered
to their allegiance, and recieved the Royal assurance
of full protection to their persons and security to
their properties;

That, at that period, throughout all His
Majestys Colonies (without any exception) a property
in Negroes was maintained and acknowledged
if not encouraged; And Your petitioners know not
of any public act since that time, whereby such
sort of property has been declared untenable = On
the contrary, the Royal Proclamations and the
acts of Parliament admitting and encouraging
persons of Your petitioners political principles to
remove out of the United States into this Province,
expressly authorise them to bring their Negro
Slaves,—

Your petitioners are far from pretending
to

Petition of John Taylor and other slaveholders, 3 December 1807. Nova Scotia Archives, Nova Scotia House of Assembly Fonds, RG 5 Series A; Volume 14, No. 49: microfilm 15591.

petitioners were born—It was authorised by the controuling authority of Parliament, in which authority the Colonists had not by representation any share—But, when your petitioners came to the age of discretion, they found that His Majestys Colonial Subjects possessed the right of holding property in Negroes upon the same grounds that they possessed the right of holding any other species of property, and [conceived] that right to be as strongly guarded by law as any other of their rights or privileges whatsoever—

But, unfortunately for your petitioners, owing to certain doubts now entertained by The Kings Courts of Law in this Province, such property is rendered wholly untenable by your petitioners, whose Negro Servants are daily leaving their service and setting your petitioners at defiance—

For, if it be no longer incumbent upon the Negro who claims his liberty within a Colony, to produce the Certificate of his emancipation; or to shew that he was born of free parents—or, at the least, to prove that at some former period of his life he exercised the rights of a free person, it is in vain that his possessor attempts to litigate with him—

Negroes, universally thro the Colonies, passed like other chattels; Sometimes by Bills of Sale, at other times by mere tradition—As in the case of other chattels, possession was a proof of property till the contrary was shewn—And your petitioners are prepared to prove their property in the Negroes they possess against all adverse claimants—But, as Negroes are transitory, Your petitioners are not (nor from the nature of the thing is it possible they should be) prepared with a legal course of testimony, for deducing such Negroes Pedigree from an African Slave ancestor,—Much less (as Colonists) are they prepared, or (as they humbly [conceive]) in reason called upon, to maintain the legality of a System which the Parliament of Great Britain has authorised, and the Parliament of the United Kingdoms doth still allow.

Leaving all subtle reasonings to better heads, your petitioners rely, and must rely, in this, as in many other cases, upon the long established usage in His Majestys Colonies, and must humbly hope for the same rule and measure of justice here, as might, in their case, be hoped for by His Majestys free colonial subjects of any other of his transmarine dominions—

Perhaps however, the peculiar circumstances of this Province, or perhaps the true interests of Humanity, may require, in this Colony, the abolition of that particular species of property claimed by your petitioners, (these however are problems that your petitioners presume not to solve) But if so, it seems but reasonable and just, that your petitioners, and others under like circumstances with them, should bear only their proportional parts of the loss or expence attending such abolition—

Upon the whole therefore,

Your petitioners confiding in the chaste manly and deliberate wisdom of this House; and fully relying upon the justice integrity and honor of this Assembly

Most humbly pray,

That their Case may be taken under Your Consideration, and that either such regulations may be made as in your wisdom shall be deemed expedient for securing your petitioners property in their Negro Servants;—Or, that, if such property is to be sacrificed to the public good, your petitioners may, from that public, receive their equitable compensation

And your petitioners as in duty bound will ever pray—

Decem, 3rd: AD. 1807
County of Annapolis

Slaveholder	Male Slaves	Female Slaves	Child Slaves
John Taylor	2	2	2
James Moody	2	1	5
Margaret Moody			1
Simeon Jones	1	1	
Isaac Hatfield	2	2	1
Henry Rutherford	1	1	2
Andrew Snodgrass	1		
Frederick Williams	2	1	3
Isaac Bonnett			2
F.L. Rohme	2		1
John Basteit		1	1
Charity Cornwell	3		
Edward Thorne	1	1	
John Vroom	1		2

Slaveholder	Male Slaves	Female Slaves	Child Slaves
Elizabeth James	1		
Nicholas James		1 [?]	3
John Polhemus	3	2	5
Mr. Winniett	2	1	1
Elijah Purdy	1	2	
Bethiah Purdy		1	
Samuel Heloson		1	1
B. Heloson		1	1
Samuel Dowset			1
Harry Dowset	1		
Frederick Devoue	1	1	
Ebenezer Cutler		1	1
Thomas Cornwell		1	2

DOCUMENT 54:
Petition of Isaac Willoughby, Former Slave, Nova Scotia, 1834[21]

Historians do not have many documents where we hear the voice of a former slave in the Maritimes. Although mediated through another person, the document provides an important insight into the troubles that black people faced in the Maritimes after gaining their freedom. Before the House could act, the petition was withdrawn for unclear reasons, but perhaps because private charities intervened. Although there were poor houses and forms of poor relief in Nova Scotia, Willoughby obviously felt entitled to some form of compensation for his many years of service as a slave.

To the Honorable the House of Assembly now convened in session at Halifax

The Petition of Isaac Willoughby Humbly Sheweth That your Petitioner who has now arrived at the age of seventy one years is induced by his peculiar circumstances of distress to solicit the aid of your Honorable House, convinced that such an appeal will not be unregarded.

That your Petitioner was born a slave and continued as such until he was 36 years of age, when he purchased his freedom, for which he paid twenty pounds and feeling desirous of procuring the freedom of his brother (who was also a slave) he paid the sum of forty pounds for that purchase, and his brother having been shortly afterwards [put] on board of a **British Man of War**, your Petitioner never received any part of the sum so advanced, and has since met with many severe losses in his struggle through life.

British Man of War: A warship or frigate belonging to the Royal Navy.

That your Petitioner's mother who was a slave also, and who is now nearly ninety years of age, was left destitute by the death of her master Jonathan Shearman [?] Esquire of the Township of Cornwallis and your Petitioner feeling the affection of a son towards a parent undertook to support and provide for her.

That your petitioner has also a wife and two children depending upon him for sustenance, and feeling that the support of his family combined with the hardships of the times, is a burthen too heavy for his advanced years, he

21 Petition of Isaac Willoughby, 8 February 1834, RG 5, Series P, NSA.

is reduced to the necessity of appealing to your Honorable House in order that you may be [inclined/induced] to grant to him such necessary aid....

Will Ever Pray,
Isaac Willoughby X his mark

Cornwallis, 10th December 1833

We the undersigned do hereby certify that the statements made in the foregoing Petition of Isaac Willoughby are to the best of our knowledge and belief substantially correct. Also that he is a sober And industrious man.

Wm. Campbell
John Wells
H. Harrington
William Allan Chipman
Elisha Dewolf

DOCUMENT 55:
Article Supporting Slavery and Decrying Free Blacks, Nova Scotia, 1842[22]

In this editorial, the author complains about the abolition of British colonial slavery, while also condemning the free black population in Nova Scotia. For some whites, the presence of free blacks hurt local society because they were perceived as a drain on the economy even though some poor whites also relied on government rations and private charities.

[The] abolition of Slavery has been a vast injury to British North America, not to speak of the deterioration of property in the Islands [the West Indies] which were victims to emancipation; or the demoralized condition of those, who, in receiving the boon of liberty, have used it in justification of insolence and inactivity. The free negro population of this province, pressing, for the most part, like a dead weight on the community, might have given England an argument that it would have been impossible to repel—of the national slothfulness of the African disposition.

---

22 *Morning Post*, 8 November 1842.

PART III

Court Cases and Bills of Sale

Court cases provide some of the most important documentary evidence about North American slavery. Although court cases must be treated with caution (obviously, the vast majority of black slaves did not end up in court), they provide important details about an individual slave's life ranging from family connections to work patterns to personality traits. Bills of sale underline how slavery commodified black people with incredible callousness.

DOCUMENT 56:
Bill of Sale, Young Boy from Maryland, Nova Scotia, 1779[1]

This document highlights the fact that slaves from southern states like Maryland were arriving in the Maritimes before the Loyalist influx in 1783. Readers should note two important aspects of this document. First, Abram is clearly being sold away from his family. We do not know whether the mother was still in Harris's household, nor who his father was (possibly Harris), but we can see that Abram is being sold alone. Second, it shows that men and women of relatively modest means could own slaves as Matthew Archibald and Matthew Harris were a tanner and farmer respectively.

Be it known to all men that I Matthew Harris of Pictou in his Majesties Province of Nova Scotia Yeoman have Bargained & sold unto Matthew Archibald of Truro within said province Tanner and I do by these presents Bargain sell alien & Convey for ever make Over to him the said Matthew Archibald his Heirs & assigns all the right property [?] or Interest I now have or at any time hereafter can pretend to have to one Negroe Boy Named Abram now about twelve years of age who was Born of my Negro slave in my House in Maryland for & in consideration of the sum of fifty pound Currancy to me ... [on this day 29 July 1779].
Matthew Harris

1 Colchester County, Register of Deeds, Vol. 1, p. 468, NSA.

DOCUMENT 57:
Bill of Sale, Mintur, 1779[2]

This is a typical bill of sale that simply lists the name of the buyer, seller, and slave along with the price. The high price indicates that Mintur was a valuable slave, probably because of his alleged physical strength. According to the Nova Scotia Archives' virtual exhibit on slavery and freedom,[3] Mintur eventually gained his freedom, married, and had a son named Freeman.

Know all by these Presents that I Joseph Northrup of Falmouth in King[s] County for and in Consideration of the sum of one hundred Pounds to me in hand from ... John Palmer of Windsor ... To Bargain and Sell unto the Said John Palmer of Windsor A negro man Named Mintur....

2 Bill of Sale, 1779, MG 100, vol. 14, # 113, NSA.

3 The exhibition can be seen at https://novascotia.ca/archives/africanns.

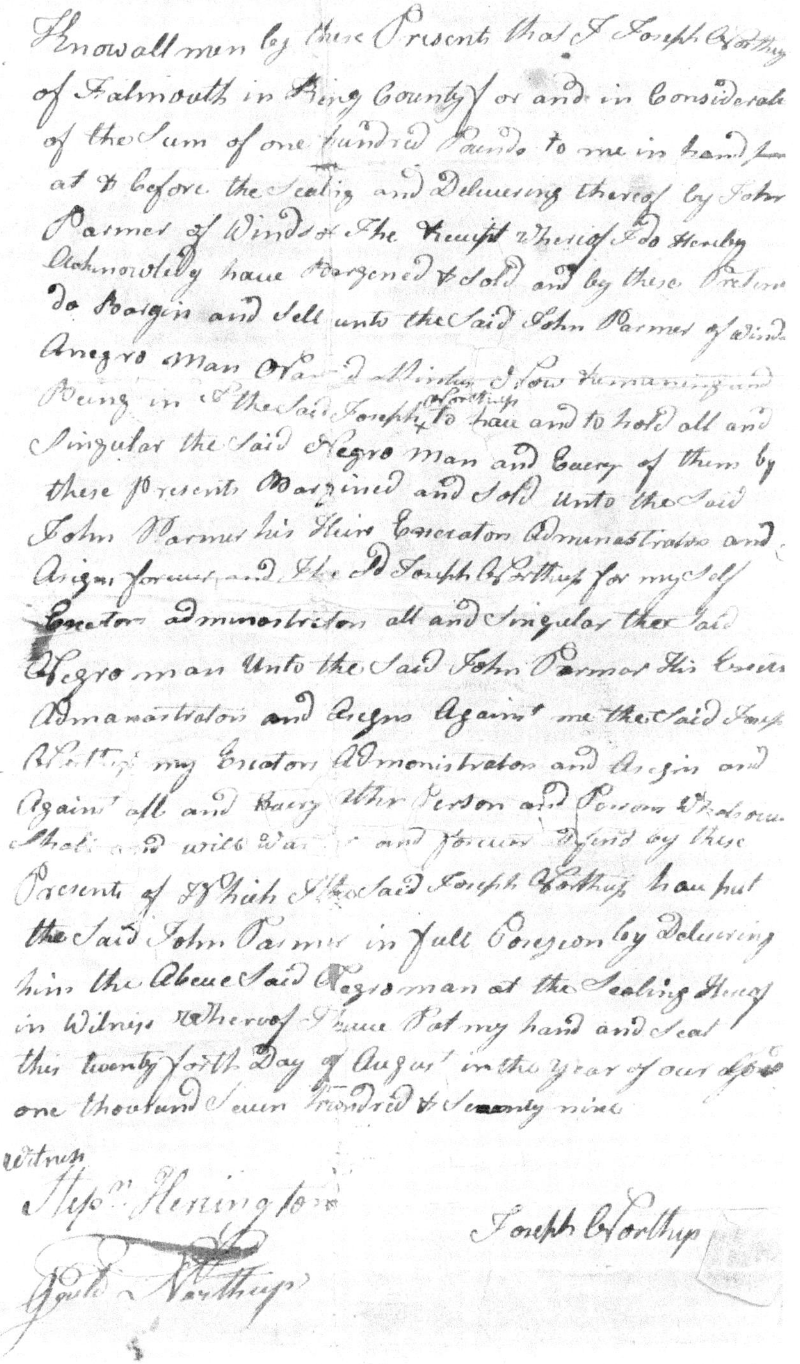
Know all men by these Presents that I Joseph Northup of Falmouth in Kings County for and in Consideration of the Sum of one hundred Pounds to me in hand paid at & before the Sealing and Delivering thereof by John Parmer of Windsor The Receipt whereof I do Hereby Acknowledge have Bargained & Sold and by these Presents do Bargain and Sell unto the Said John Parmer of Windsor A negro Man Named Mintur Now Remaining and Being in the Said Joseph Northup to have and to hold all and Singular the Said Negro Man and Every of them by these Presents Bargained and Sold unto the Said John Parmer his Heirs Executors Administrators and Assigns forever and I the Sd Joseph Northup for my Self Executors administrators all and Singular the Said Negro man unto the Said John Parmer his Executors Administrators and Assigns Against me the Said Joseph Northup my Executors Administrators and Assigns and Against all and Every other Person and Persons Whatsoever Shall and will Warrant and forever Defend by these Presents of Which I the Said Joseph Northup have put the Said John Parmer in full Possession by Delivering him the Above Said Negro man at the Sealing thereof in Witness Whereof I have Set my hand and Seal this twenty forth Day of August in the year of our Lord one thousand Seven hundred & Seventy nine

Witness
Stepn. Henington
[illegible] Northup

Joseph Northup

Sale of slave "Mintur" by Joseph Northrup to Joseph Palmer in Windsor, 1779. Nova Scotia Archives, Miscellaneous Manuscripts Collection, MG 100; Volume 14, No. 113: microfilm 794.

DOCUMENT 58:

R. v. Jesse Gray, for Whipping Pero 100 Times, Nova Scotia, 1786[4]

A Southern Loyalist, Jesse Gray brought a few other black people to Nova Scotia and probably re-enslaved them. His treatment of Mary Postell and her children would become one of the most famous cases related to slavery in the history of Nova Scotian jurisprudence (see Document 59, p. 107). The Pero Davis incident is an indication of Gray's brutality toward black people. Despite Davis's deposition, the grand jury ultimately decided to dismiss the charges.

County of Shelburne

Personally Appeard this fifth day of November 1786 Pero Davis who being Sworn did Depose and say that sum time in the month of May Last the day he Does not Recolect, he being out [in] Argyle in said County in the Imploy of one Jesse Gray, he was by the said Jesse Gray Most Severly Beat with a Cowskin to the number of one hundred Lashes Round his Body in the gratest violence he Could Lay on in so much that he Cut the body of the Deponent in several Places—

Sworne this fifth
Day of November
1786 Before me
Valentine Nutter
Justice of the Peace

Pero Davis his mark

4 *R. v. Jesse Gray*, 9 November 1786, Shelburne, vol. 27, no. 27.2, RG 60, NSA.

DOCUMENT 59:
Mary Postell Affidavit, Nova Scotia, 1791[5]

The most famous (or infamous) case of re-enslavement is that of Mary Postell and her children. Unlike most aspects of the history of Maritime slavery, this particular incident has received sustained attention. The African Nova Scotian scholar Sylvia Hamilton memorialized Postell in a poem entitled "Potato Lady," while Carole Troxler has published an excellent essay about her sad life.[6] The case is rare in that there is clear documentation that demonstrates re-enslavement and cruelty, but it also illustrates the ways in which black people attempted to negotiate their way out of bondage. The story highlights the evil treatment of a mother and her brutally imposed separation from her children. In 1791, Mary Postell went to the court and "Complained against Jesse Gray, of Argyle, for taking away her children."

The indictment against Jesse Gray included the details of his re-enslavement and treatment of Mary Postell and her children by indicating that in 1785 Jesse Gray had violated the King's peace by enslaving Mary Postell and her two children, Flora and Nelly (also called Nell), in St. Augustine, Florida, and Shelburne, Nova Scotia. Gray, the indictment continued, through a combination of "grievous threatenings and other enormous abuses [did] compell terrify and oblige [the three] to serve, Work, and Labour" for his profit. Gray forced Mary Postell and her children into "the Hold of the said Ship or Vessel called the *Spring* Transport upon the High Seas for a long space of Time," and after 25 days they landed at Shelburne. For the next two years, Gray forced Mary Postell and her children to "Work and Labour ... as the Slave and Slaves of him." The court papers also noted that Gray had set an "Evil Example of all others offending in the like kind." After exploiting Postell and her children, Gray decided to sell her to William Mangham for "One Hundred Bushels of Potatoes." In 1790, Gray sold Flora Postell to John Henderson for £5. Henderson then took the child, around nine or ten years old, to North Carolina.[7]

The case hinged on the testimony given by Mary Postell, Jesse Gray, and others. Mary Postell told the court that she had been born in South Carolina and was the "property of a certain Elijah Postell." After Elijah Postell's death,

---

5 *R. v. Gray*, April to November 1791, Shelburne County Court of General Sessions of the Peace, RG 60, vol. 1, # 49.4, NSA.

6 Sylvia Hamilton, "Potato Lady," in George Elliott Clarke, ed., *Fire on the Water: An Anthology of Black Nova Scotian Writing*, vol. 2 (Lawrencetown: Pottersfield Press 1992); Carole Watterson Troxler, "Re-enslavement of Black Loyalists: Mary Postell in South Carolina, East Florida, and Nova Scotia," *Acadiensis* 37 (Summer/Fall, 2008): 70–85.

7 *R. v. Gray*, April to November 1791.

Mary became the slave of his son, who served in the Continental army during the war. She "joined" British forces near Charleston and evacuated to St. Augustine and eventually reached Shelburne with Jesse Gray, who promised to "use her well." Postell stated that Gray, "has no right whatever to her or her Children and that she is afraid that said Jesse Gray or William Mangham will seize her and Child and carry them away."[8] In support of Postell, Scipio and Dinah Wearing testified that Mr. Postell had owned Mary. Dinah claimed that Postell had run away from her owner and came into British lines (meaning she should have been free). Scipio stated that Postell had been employed in public works for the British. Significantly, Dinah further pointed out that she had never known anyone else to own Mary Postell aside from the Postell family.[9]

In his defence, Jesse Gray claimed that he had originally purchased Mary and her child Flora from Joseph Rea (or Wray) of Virginia in St. Augustine in 1783. Gray claimed that he then sold Mary and Flora to his brother Samuel Gray. Allegedly, Mary and Flora lived with Samuel for about two years, during which time Mary gave birth to her younger daughter Nell. At this point, Gray purchased Mary and her children from his brother and migrated to Shelburne. Gray also admitted that he sold Mary to William Mangham and her daughter Flora to John Henderson. But he kept Nell at his house.[10] Gray obtained the support of a few witnesses. Not surprisingly, William Mangham stated that he had purchased Mary in 1787 for the hundred bushels of potatoes. He also mentioned knowing that Jesse Gray had a bill of sale from Samuel Gray. Gray also called Margaret Harris who lived in East Florida. She claimed that Mary Postell wanted Harris's husband to purchase Mary and her daughter Flora.

The Court decided that the defendant was not guilty. Gray had been originally charged with a misdemeanour: that he was not the owner of Mary Postell and her children. Simply stated, Postell did not prove that she had been a free person.[11] The decision to return Mary Postell to slavery underlined the presumption that a black person was a slave unless proven otherwise. That Postell was re-enslaved, however, should not obscure for readers the way she pressed her claim as far as possible. In the years after the Postell decision, Nova Scotia judges reversed the course set by the Postell case. Instead of forcing alleged slaves to prove they were free, slave-owners had to prove that they had the legal right to hold slaves—which, for many, turned out to be difficult or impossible.

---

8 *Idem.*

9 Shelburne Records, MG 4, vol. 141, NSA.

10 *Idem.*

11 *Idem.*

County of Shelburne
Shelburne

Mary Postell of Shelburne a Negro Woman Maketh Oath upon the Holy Evangelist of Almighty God. That she was born in South Carolina and was the property of a certain Elijah Postell. That after the death of the said Elijah she became the property of William the son of the said Elijah who was a Captain in the American Army then in Rebellion [against] Great Britain That she joined the **King's Troops** near Charlestown and when that place was evacuated went to Saint Augustine and came from thence to Shelburne with [a certain?] Jesse Gray who promised to use her well whilst she would live with him That sometime after her arrival here the said Jesse Gray (who now resides at Argyle) [took] her two Children and did actually dispose of her to a certain William Mangham and also sold and disposed of her oldest girl (aged about 10 years) to one John Henderson who carried her to South Carolina [or North Carolina] as she is informed, [Gray intends to] sell her youngest Child—and this deponent [?] sayeth that said Jesse Gray has no right whatever to her as her Children and that she is afraid that said Jesse Gray or William Mangham will seize her & her child & carry them away—

King's Troops: This generally refers to people who fought against the Patriots during the American Revolution.

DOCUMENT 60:

Grand Jury Complaint, Re-enslavement of Black Boy Sent to the West Indies Illegally, Nova Scotia, 1794[12]

This is yet another example of how indentured servitude could easily become re-enslavement. In this case, a white Nova Scotian sold a boy into slavery in the West Indies. This example should be put in the context of the other examples of re-enslavement in this book.

Gentlemen

We have this day receiv'd information that a Negro Boy formerly bound to John Stuart, & by him transferr'd, to some person in Liverpool, has lately been Carried off to the West Indies. & left Bound (as it is said) to some person there.

The Grand Jury earnestly request the Worship full Bench would write to the Justices in Liverpool for information on this Subject, as a transaction of this nature (independent of its illegality) if Overlook'd, will be productive of much injury to the Community in preventing the Negroes from Binding out their Children in future.

Shelburne
April 22. 1794

By Order of the Grand Jury
James Cox, Foreman.

12 Black Boy Carried Off, 22 April 1794, Shelburne County Court of General Sessions of the Peace, RG 34-321, J 145, NSA.

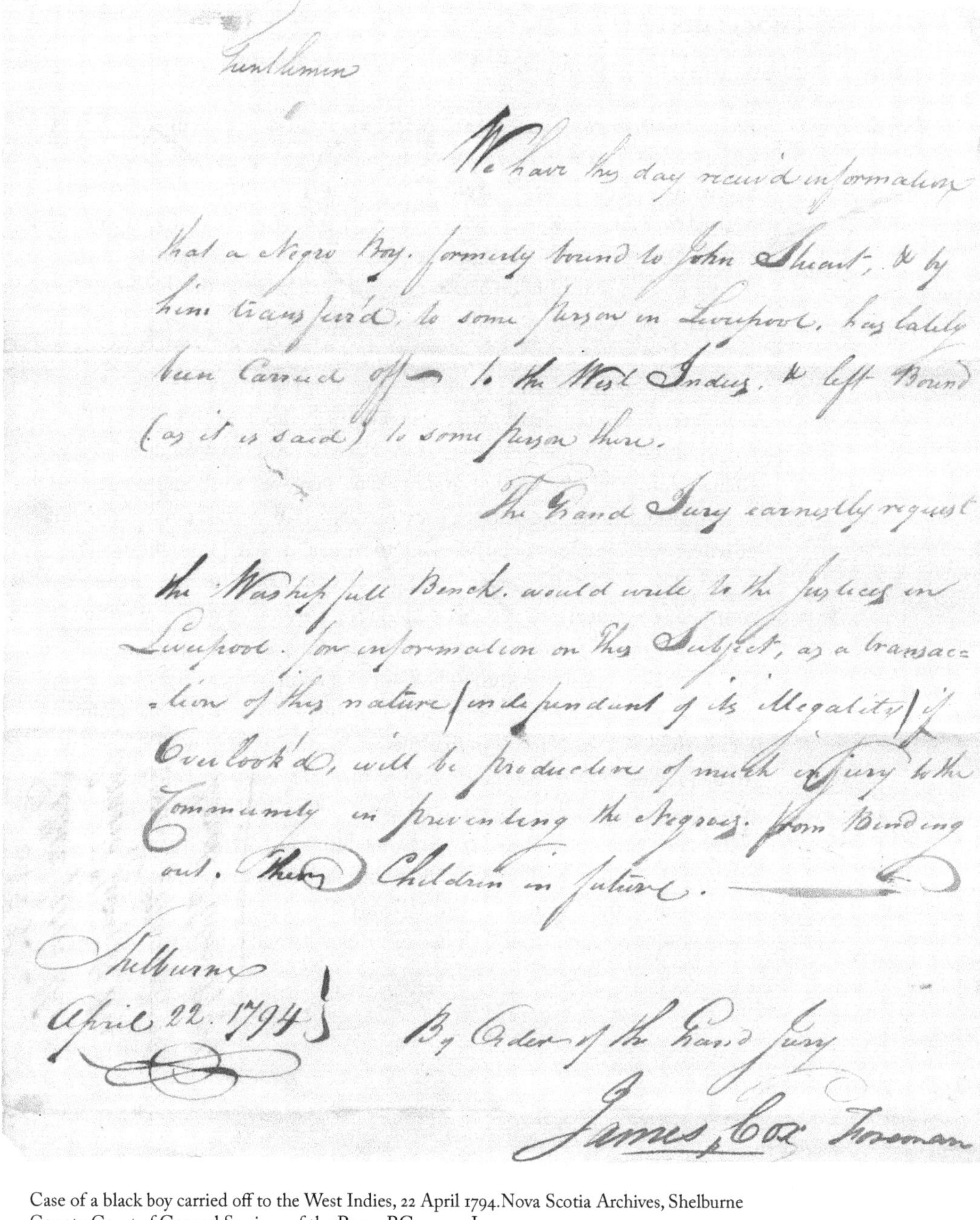

Gentlemen

We have this day received information that a Negro Boy. formerly bound to John Stuart, & by him transferr'd to some person in Liverpool, has lately been Carried off to the West Indies, & left Bound (as it is said) to some person there.

The Grand Jury earnestly request the Worshipfull Bench. would write to the Justices in Liverpool. for information on this Subject, as a transaction of this nature (independant of its Illegality) if Overlook'd, will be productive of much Injury to the Community in preventing the Negroes. from Binding out. Their Children in future.

Shelburne
April 22. 1794

By Order of the Grand Jury
James Cox Foreman

Case of a black boy carried off to the West Indies, 22 April 1794.Nova Scotia Archives, Shelburne County Court of General Sessions of the Peace, RG 34-321, J145.

DOCUMENT 61:
James DeLancey Complaint Against William Woodin, 1803[13]

DeLancey v. Woodin is perhaps the most celebrated slave case in Nova Scotia history. James DeLancey was one of the more aggressive slaveholders in Nova Scotia. According to Joseph Aplin (Document 51, p. 91), who was the junior counsel for DeLancey, "Jack, who was legally the slave of Col. DeLancey at New York, accompanied his master to London on the Evacuation of the former Place. From London [he went with] his Master to this Province." In 1800, after years of enslavement, Jack absconded from his owner and went to Halifax. It seems that Jack hoped to enlist in the Royal Nova Scotia Regiment or believed that he would become free simply by escaping to Halifax. After DeLancey found out that William Woodin had employed Jack, he had his lawyer Thomas Ritchie demand that the slave be returned. Woodin's lawyer, Richard John Uniacke, refused, arguing that there was no statute law related to slavery and so all blacks in the province were free. At this point, "an action of **trover** was commenced by Mr. DeLancey against Mr. [Woodin] for the Negro Slave."[14] DeLancey won the case in the Annapolis annual circuit court, but the judgement was arrested. As it turned out, a new trial set for September 1803 did not occur and DeLancey did not "obtain execution of his judgment against Woodin."[15] DeLancey died in May 1804. Although no judgement had been entered regarding DeLancey, many slaveholders took his failure to recover Jack as a sign that the courts would not uphold slaveholding in the province. One important aspect of this case lies in the role that Jack played in freeing himself. By running away, Jack took his own freedom. Of course, the legal system could have returned him to slavery—thanks to the work of Uniacke and others it did not—but Jack took the original risk of running away and forcing the issue to court. The case of *DeLancey v. Woodin* could not have happened if Jack had not run away and attempted to enlist.

trover: A claim to obtain damages for the wrongful use of one's property.

13 *DeLancey v. Woodin*, 1803, RG 39 C, Vol. 1, #2, NSA.

14 *Opinions of Several Gentlemen*, 5.

15 Barry Cahill, "Slavery and the Judges of Loyalist Nova Scotia," *University of New Brunswick Law Journal* 43 (1994): 73–135.

Nova Scotia Sup Court
At Annapolis
Michaelmas Term in the
Forty third year of the reign
Of King George the Third

Annapolis [?] James DeLancey complains of William Woodin ... that whereas one Jack a Negro Man, on the first day of may in the year of our Lord one thousand eight hundred at Annapolis in the County of Annapolis aforesaid was lawfully obtained in the service of the said James DeLancey as his slave and servant to serve him the said James DeLancey for and during the natural life of the said Jack ... willfully and without the leave or license and against the will of the said James DeLancey departed and deserted himself from [James DeLancey for the service of] William Woodin. Yet the said William Woodin well knowing the said Jack to be the slave and servant of the said James DeLancey as a slave and servant, but continuing to injure the said James DeLancey and to deprive him of the benefit and service of the said Jack his slave and servant....

James DeLancey during the whole time aforesaid lost not only the service of the said Jack his slave and servant, but also many great profits and advantages which he might have had and gained, if the aforesaid William Woodin had not received and kept the aforesaid Jack into his service: wherefore this said James DeLancey says he is injured and hath sustained damages to the value of five hundred pounds and therefore he brings suit.

DOCUMENT 62:
Supreme Court Case "Nancy," New Brunswick, 1800[16]

In 1800, the issue of the status of a slave woman was brought before the court in the cases *R. v. Jones* and *R. v. Agnew*. The first case involved a woman named "Ann otherwise called Nancy" whom Jones had brought from Maryland in 1785. The second case involved one of Stair Agnew's female slaves. Both cases began at the same time, but once a decision was rendered in *R. v. Jones* the other case did not proceed.[17] The slave woman in *R. v. Jones* probably attempted to escape from Jones in 1786 and he described her as "about 24 years old, who took with her a Negro child about four years old called LIDGE" (see Document 19, p. 47). In the summer of 1799, a writ of ***habeas corpus*** was "brought by a Negro woman claimed as a Slave by Captain Jones of Fredericton, in order to procure her liberation."[18] During the trial, the "question of Slavery upon general principles was discussed at great length." After hearing the testimony, the court remained divided and did not reach a judgement. As a result, Caleb Jones obtained Nancy because the divided court did not enter a judgement. The 1800 non-decision is noteworthy because all of the judges either owned slaves in New Brunswick or had possessed them in the United States.

habeas corpus: Literally, "that you have the body" (Latin). A writ of *habeas corpus* may be used to bring someone before a court of law in order to determine whether their detention (typically as a prisoner, but in this case as a slave) is legal.

New-Brunswick.
SAINT JOHN,
TUESDAY, February 18.

Last week the Hilary Term of the Supreme Court was held at Fredericton, at which we understand there were few causes agitated of any consequence excepting one upon an Habeas Corpus brought by a Negro Woman claimed as a slave by Captain Jones of Fredericton, in order to procure her liberation. The question of Slavery upon general principles was discussed at great length, by the Counsel on both sides, and we understand the Court were divided in their opinions, the Chief Justice and Judge Upham being of opinion that by the existing Law of this Province, Negroes may be held as Slaves here, and Judge Allen and Judge Saunders being of opinion, that the Law upon that subject is the same here as in England and therefore that Slavery is not recognized by the Laws of this Province.—The Court being thus divided, no judgment was entered.

---

16 *Royal Gazette*, 18 February 1800.

17 D.G. Bell, "Slavery and the Judges of Loyalist New Brunswick," *University of New Brunswick Law Journal* 31 (1982): 9–42; W.A. Spray, "Jones, Caleb," *Dictionary of Canadian Biography*.

18 *Royal Gazette*, 18 February 1800.

DOCUMENT 63:
Ward Chipman's Slavery Brief, New Brunswick Supreme Court, 1800[19]

This document is a small excerpt of Solicitor General Ward Chipman's lengthy brief to the New Brunswick Supreme Court opposing slavery during the 1800 Nancy Case (see previous document). Five years later, Chipman argued a case from a pro-slavery perspective. In this excerpt, Chipman highlights how gradual emancipation took place on a private level between individual owners and slaves with slaves becoming indentured servants for a few years before gaining their complete freedom.

That some masters have brought slaves here is true, and that the Slaves have in some instances continued with their Masters, without disputing the right of their masters to their service is also true.—But it must also be admitted that the Slaves have in many instances controverted this right, and have been manumitted, or indented themselves voluntarily to serve for a term of years upon condition of being discharged at the expiration of it.

19 Ward Chipman, Supreme Court New Brunswick, Hilary Term 1800. 40. Geo. 3 *The Case of Nancy a black woman, claimed as a Slave; upon Habeas Corpus against the Master.*

DOCUMENT 64:

R. v. Andrews (Indictment of Samuel Andrews Jr.), Slave-Owners Murder a Female Slave, Yarmouth, Nova Scotia, 1801[20]

At the turn of the century, Nova Scotia master Samuel Andrews Jr. murdered a female slave named Jude or Judy by beating her with sticks. Although he was indicted for murder, the court acquitted him (along with his father and brother) of the crime despite overwhelming medical evidence that revealed that a blunt object had been used to kill her. Jude's sister Diana testified against Andrews but the testimony of a black female slave meant nothing to the jury.

The Jurors for our Lord the King upon their Oath that Samuel Andrews junior late of Yarmouth in the County of Shelburne Yeomen not having the fear of God before his eyes but being moved and seduced by the instigation of the Devil ... did strike Beat & Kick giving to the said Jude as well by the casting and throwing of her the said Jude to the Ground aforesaid as also by stricking beating and kicking the said Jude in and Upon the Head Stomach Back and sides of Her the said Jude with the stick aforesaid and with both the Hands and feet of Him ... [causing] several Mortal Wounds [from which she died].

20 *R. v. Andrews*, 19 May 1801, Shelburne County Special Court of Oyer and Terminer, RG 42 SH vol. 1 file 4, NSA.

DOCUMENT 65:

Slave Returned to Owner, Supreme Court, Prince Edward Island, 1802[21]

Prince Edward Island remained the only part of the Maritimes that had **statute law** recognizing slavery. The 1781 Slave Baptism Act had legalized slavery and would not be overturned until an 1825 Repeal Act. As a result, the Supreme Court of Prince Edward Island returned Sam to bondage because slavery had legal recognition.

statute law: Written law passed by legislative authority. As discussed in the Introduction, there was no statute law recognizing slavery in Nova Scotia or New Brunswick.

Friday the second day of July 1802 the court met.

A Negro named Sam brought up by Habeas Corpus calling on Thos. Wright Esq. to bring into court the Body of the said Negro together with the Cause of his detention—In obedience to which the said Thos. Wright personally appears and brings into Court the Body of the said Negro and produces a Bill of Sale of him from John Strickland to himself. It is ordered by the court that the said Negro return to service of his said Master [whose] Title to him appears perfect and compleat.

21 Supreme Court, Prince Edward Island, RG 6.1, Series I, Sub-series I, vol. 10, 49, PAROPEI.

DOCUMENT 66:

Bill of Sale for Percilla, Eight-Year-Old Girl, Nova Scotia, 1804[22]

In this document, the estate of a deceased man sold a very young slave girl. What is telling about this document is the very indifferent, cold, and calculating way the document describes selling such a young child. Not surprisingly, no mention is made of the girl's father or mother.

THIS INDENTURE made the sixth day of October one thousand eight hundred and four, BETWEEN Jane Dickson, William Prince, and Isaac Bennett of Annapolis, County of Annapolis and Province of Nova Scotia, administratrix and administrators of the goods and Chattels, Rights and Credits which [were] of Robert Dickson late of the same place Esquire Deceased of the one part, and William Robertson of the same place merchant of the other part, WITNESSETH ... for and in consideration of the sum of seventeen pounds lawful money of Nova Scotia to them in hand paid by the said William Robertson ... [for] ... a certain Negro Girl slave named Percilla about eight years and four months of age being part of the personal estate of the said Robert Dickson deceased.

22 Sale of a Slave, MG 100, vol. 103, #F3a, NSA.

DOCUMENT 67:
Supreme Court Case, Newspaper Account, New Brunswick, 1806[23]

In 1805, the anti-slavery attorney Samuel Denny Street went before the New Brunswick Supreme Court and filed for a writ of *habeas corpus* for Richard Hopefield, Jr., who had allegedly been detained by Stair Agnew "for the space of Three years and fifty five Days." The case focused on Patience (also known as Stacey or Statia) who had been brought to New Brunswick as a slave, eventually married Richard Hopefield Sr., and had several children, including the younger Hopefield whom Agnew claimed to own. During the case, Hopefield Sr. gave a deposition that outlined his personal life history. Born in Virginia, Hopefield served his owner during the Revolutionary War before escaping to the British. Shortly thereafter, he married Patience and had several children including Richard Hopefield Jr., who was born in New Brunswick. Hopefield claimed that his wife "had been put on board a vessel by one Phineas Lovitt [a member of the House of Assembly] in order as the deponent was informed to send her to the West Indies to be sold—when she was relanded by order of Governor Carleton who set her at liberty." It seems that Patience and Hopefield lived together for several years as free people before Joseph Clarke "forcibly seized" her.[24] In 1792, Joseph Clarke placed an advertisement in a local paper complaining about the loss of a female slave named "STATIA" and her five-year-old son and fifteen-month-old daughter. Clarke also noted that she had run away with an indentured servant named Dick Hopewell (probably Richard Hopefield) who claimed to be married to Statia (see Document 30, p. 58). Clarke recovered his property and sold her to Joseph Hewlett.

Stair Agnew denied the charges against him and benefited from the advice and legal representation of Ward Chipman, who admitted that his client had beaten Hopefield Jr., but claimed it resulted from "disobedient and refractory and insolent" behaviour and neglect of "duty." Agnew did not dispute that he prevented "Richard from absenting himself." Agnew justified his actions, however, because Richard was "a Negro Servant, the property of the said Stair ... bound to serve the said Stair for his the said Richard's life time."[25] Agnew's claims were damaged by the testimony of other witnesses. In 1801, the York County Court of General Sessions had indicted him for "Cruel Treatment" of "two Negro Boys" in his service. At the court, Agnew "publickly pledged"

---

23 *Royal Gazette*, 10 September 1806.

24 *Richard Hopefield v. Stair Agnew*, 1802/1805, RS 42, Supreme Court Original Jurisdiction Records, PANB.

25 *Idem.*

that "he would manumitt and make free a certain Negro Boy named or called Richard Hopefield" when he turned 21 years old.[26]

Samuel Denny Street argued that since Hopefield Sr. was a free man, his son ought to be free as well. The defence "countered by attempting to show that Hopefield's parents had never been formally married, so that he had taken the status of his mother rather than of his [free] father."[27] After a court battle, Hopefield's writ of *habeas corpus* failed. Also, a civil suit against Agnew for battery and false imprisonment did not proceed past an early stage.[28] In sum, Hopefield's case for freedom had failed. As historian David Bell notes, "Hopefield's case was undoubtedly a legal triumph for the slave-owning interests. They had received a clear legal verdict in favour of the continuance of Negro slavery."[29]

In 1806, Joseph Clarke brought an action of trover against anti-slavery attorney Samuel Denny Street "for a *Negro Boy* claimed by the Plaintiff as his *Slave*." One of Clarke's slaves had run away and found shelter with Street, who refused to give the slave back to his owner. At the trial, the plaintiff provided a bill of sale from Gabriel Fowler, who had brought the boy's mother to New Brunswick after the War. The boy had been born in New Brunswick and his father was free. Denny's attorney moved for a non-suit on four grounds. First, there was not enough evidence to establish that the mother of the boy was actually a slave. Second, the father was born free and the son's condition should follow that of the father, not the mother. Third, "there was no Law of this Province creative of Slavery." Lastly, the action of trover did not apply because no person could claim property in a slave. The newspaper account of the trial noted that, "the general question of Slavery was not agitated." The Chief Justice believed that legal title to the mother had been established, but directed the non-suit based on the third and fourth arguments of Street's lawyer.

1. The first was an action of *Trover* brought by JOSEPH CLARKE, Esq., against SAMUEL D. STREET, Esq., for a *Negro Boy* claimed by the Plaintiff as his *Slave*. The Plaintiff gave in evidence a bill of sale from one *Gabriel Fowler* to him for the mother of the Boy in question, and a permit

26 *Richard Hopefield v. Stair Agnew*; Bell, "Judges of Loyalist New Brunswick," 24–25.

27 Bell, "Judges of Loyalist New Brunswick," 24.

28 *Idem.*, 25.

29 *Idem.*, 25.

from the Police Office of New-York dated in 1783, to *Fowler* to bring the Woman as his Slave to this Country.

—It appeared that the Boy was born at or near the City of Saint John after the date of the bill of sale, and that his father, (if known) was a *freeman*; that he had run away from the Plaintiff, and was harboured by the Defendant. The conversion was satisfactorily proved by an *implied* refusal to deliver the Boy upon demand. The Counsel for the Defendant moved for a Nonsuit upon four grounds, viz.

1st.—That it did not sufficiently appear that the mother of the Boy was a Slave. (For the general question of Slavery was not agitated.)

2d.—That it appeared that the Boy was a bastard, or otherwise [that his father was a free man; and in either case he must be free, as by the Laws of] England, the issue follows the condition of the *father* and not the mother.

3d.—That as there was no Law of this Province creative of Slavery, and its existence here depended wholly upon the several Acts of the British Parliament, which were silent as to the *Children* born of Slaves, they could not be held in Slavery, but were entitled, as British subjects, born in this Province, to all the benefits of the Common Law of England, which is the Law of this Country; and therefore, admitting that the Rule of the Civil Law "*that the child follows the condition of the mother*," should prevail, or that both the Parents of the Boy were African Slaves, he being a native of this Province must be free.

4th.—That the action of *Trover* would not lie for a *Negro Slave*, because no person could have that *uncontrouled* and *unlimited property* in a *Slave*, which was necessary to support this action.

The Counsel for the Plaintiff urged in reply, that an action like this had been brought in *Nova-Scotia* by Mr. De Lancey; and quoted the opinion of Mr. *Aplin*, supported by several learned Gentlemen in England, (as appeared by a Pamphlet published in this Province,) but the Chief Justice did not think that case of sufficient authority, and directed the Nonsuit, upon the third and fourth grounds moved by the defendant. His Honour was of opinion that the title to the mother was sufficiently established, and as to the second he was silent.

PART IV

Government Documents

Government documents offer readers the opportunity to explore legislation related to slavery ranging from unpassed bills to Prince Edward Island's Slave Baptism Act. These sources illuminate how government officials ranging from the Lieutenant Governor to other officials understood and dealt with slavery.

DOCUMENT 68:
Governor Cornwallis Discusses Captain Bloss and His Slaves, 1750[1]

In this document, Governor Cornwallis mentions the large holding of slaves that Captain Bloss brought to Nova Scotia. Historians do not know much about these slaves and what happened to them. Some scholars believe that the slaves sold to Boston from Halifax in 1751 included some of these people (see Document 1, p. 24).

Captain Bloss a half pay Captain of Man of War is come here has brought with him sixteen negroes, has built a very good house at his own expense, is a sensible worthy man, he is going to pass some accounts that is necessary being abroad many years.

1 Letter from Governor Cornwallis about Captain Bloss, RG 1, vol. 35, doc. 25, NSA.

DOCUMENT 69:

An Act, *declaring that* Baptism *of* SLAVES *shall not exempt them from* BONDAGE, Prince Edward Island, 1781[2]

This act about slave baptism is the only piece of legislation in the Maritimes that acknowledged the legality of slavery. The authors of this bill probably hoped it would encourage slaveholders from the American colonies and other British possessions to consider moving to the small Island.

An act Declaring that Baptism of Slaves Shall not Exempt them from Bondage.—

Whereas some Doubts have arisen,—whether Slaves admitted to Baptism, should by Virtue thereof be made free.—

Be it therefore Enacted By His Excellency the Governor, Council, and House of Representatives in this present General Assembly and by the authority of the same. It is hereby Enacted that the conferring of Baptism, on Blacks, or Mullatoes, Doth not alter their condition, but that they shall continue to be slaves;—notwithstanding they should by the Permission of their Masters, Mistresses, [otherwise?] become Christians.

And, Be it Enacted by the authority aforesaid; That all Black and Mullatoe Servants Imported into this Island, being Slaves, shall continue as such, unless Emancipated by their Owners.—

And, Be it Enacted by the authority aforesaid that [all?] the Children Born of Women Slaves [shall?] belong to, and be the Property of the Masters, or Mistresses of said Mothers.—

Passed the 12th March 1781

2 An Act, *declaring that* Baptism *of* SLAVES *shall not exempt them from* BONDAGE, 1781, CO 228, Colonial Office Acts No. 1, Prince Edward Island, 1770–1781, MS. 1–66, PAROPEI.

DOCUMENT 70:
Book of Negroes[3]

The Book of Negroes is a list of thousands of African Americans who left the American colonies for the Maritimes, Quebec, and other regions throughout the British Empire at the conclusion of the Revolutionary War (1783). Although the majority of names in the Book of Negroes are those who

3 Book of Negroes, Sir Guy Carleton Papers, National Archives, microfilm copy at NSA.

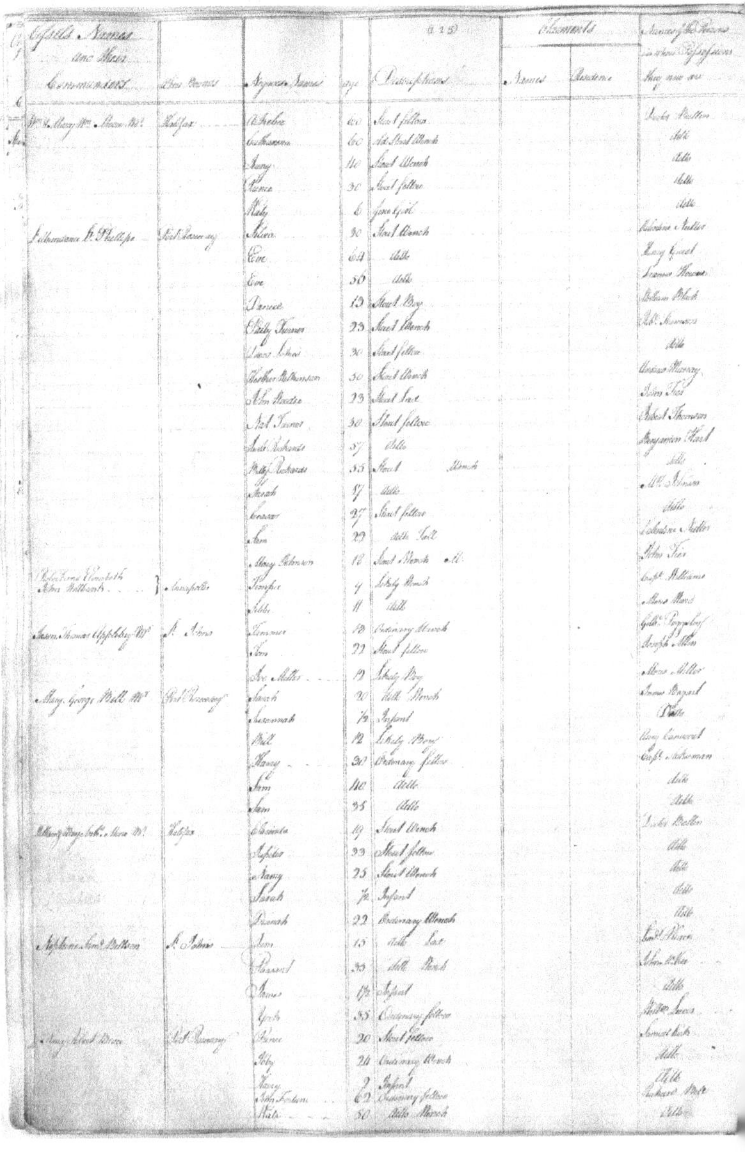

obtained their freedom during the war, it also contains the names of slaves. The document includes an individual black person's name, age, sex, and a description of how they came to British lines. Once under British protection, most former slaves were given General Birch Certificates (GBC) denoting their freedom. Often, historians have used the Book of Negroes to examine the Black Loyalists or those who gained freedom during the Revolution. This otherwise valuable approach has left out the hundreds of black people who were listed as slaves and suffered continued enslavement in the Maritimes and Quebec.

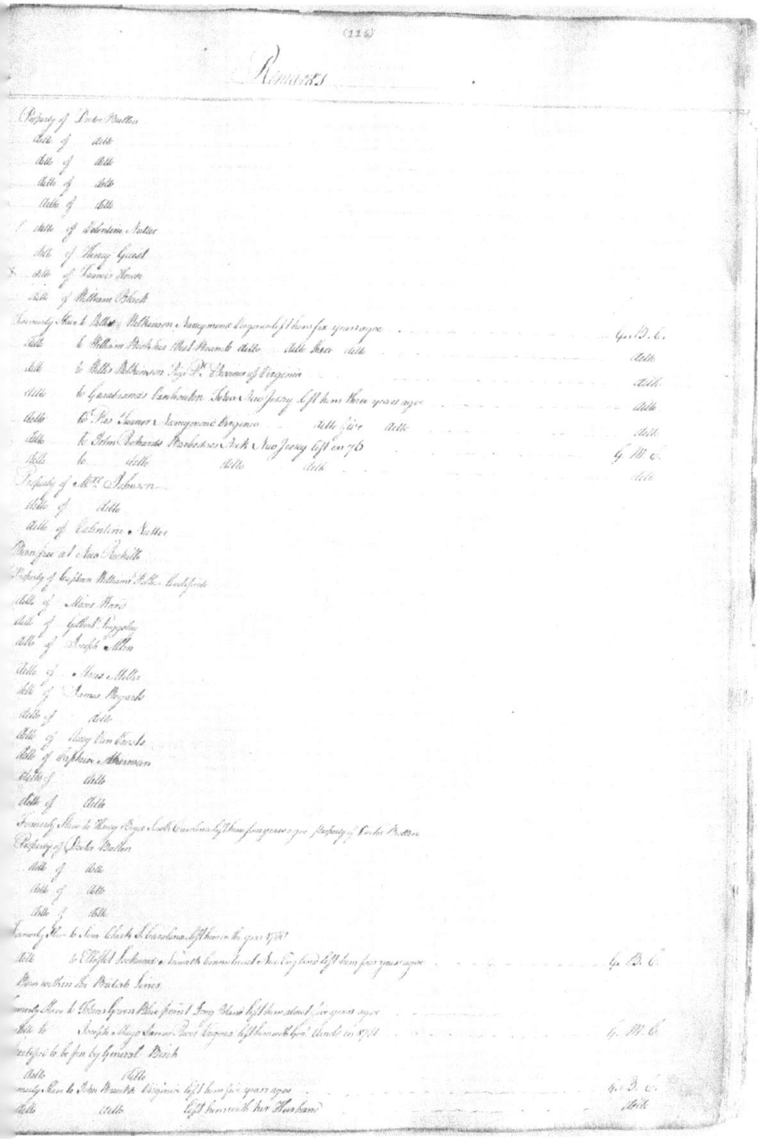
(116)

Remarks

DOCUMENT 71:

Dick Hill, Re-Enslaved, Shelburne, Nova Scotia, 1787[4]

In 1787, a free black man named Dick Hill had been unlawfully placed on board a schooner to be sent to the West Indies as a slave. Incredibly, Hill had a General Birch Certificate, which allegedly guaranteed his freedom. Unfortunately, the historical record is full of other examples of black people who, like Dick Hill, were re-enslaved and sold to the West Indies.

Capt. McDonald

There is Negro put on Board your [vessel] by the name of Dick Hill, it appears that this Negro is a Free Man and came to Novascotia by Virtue of a Pass from Genl. Birch, you must therefore not take this Negro away But send him on Shore for examination, as you will be answerable in case the Negro is taken away.—

Gregory Springall, JP

Immediately upon hearing of the Complaint of the Negro being put on Board Capt. McDonald, and the free pass of Genl Birch produced, a letter was wrote to Capt McDonald to send the Negro on Shore, but the Vessell was got underway and almost out of the Harbour.

4 Paper Respecting Dick Hill, a Free Negro Man sent to West Indies from Shelburne in Joshua Wise's Schooner Commanded by Captain McDonald, 1787, Shelburne, #25.3, RG 60, NSA.

DOCUMENT 72:

An Act for the Regulation & Relief of the Free Negroes within the Province of Nova Scotia (Unpassed), 1789[5]

In the absence of a slave code, slaveholders in Nova Scotia understood the frailty of their claims to ownership. This unpassed bill is one example of a series of efforts to secure statutory recognition for slavery within the province. Maritime slaveholders attempted to gain legal protections for slavery in 1787, 1789, 1801 (in New Brunswick and Nova Scotia), and 1808. Disguised as an attempt to regulate free black people, the bill sought to canonize, assert, and uphold slaveholder's right to own slaves. The bill also admitted that black people were regularly kidnapped and sent to slavery in Jamaica, Barbados, and other Caribbean islands. (Please note this is an extract from the original bill and not the entire document).

Whereas the free Negroes residing in this Province are daily increasing, and many inconveniences are likely to arise if the strictest good order and regularity be not observed among that class of people, and Whereas upon every principle of justice and humanity they are entitled, equally with the rest of the community, to every right and privilege of British Subjects, and no person or persons whatsoever can by authority of Law enslave them unless they are proved by Birth or otherwise to be bound to servitude for life, and Whereas attempts have been made to carry some of them out of the Province, by force and stratagem, for the scandalous purpose of making property of them in the West Indies contrary to their will and consent, for preventing whereof,

Be it Enacted by the Lieut:Governor Council and Assembly

That from and after the publication hereof all Negroes residing within this province who are not Slaves by Birth or otherwise and who shall be convicted before any three Justices of the County in which such Negro shall be found of not having a fixed place of abode or a proper means of Subsistence, or of being an idle disorderly person, it shall and may be lawful for such Justices to bind by Indenture said Negro or Negroes, without his or their consent, to any person or persons whatsoever for any term not exceeding seven years, provided that the Master or Mistress of the said

5 An Act for the Regulation and Relief of the Free Negroes within the Province of Nova Scotia, In Council, 2 April 1789, RG 5, Series U, Un-passed Bills, 1762–1792, NSA.

Negroes shall not transport nor carry them out of the Province upon pain of incurring the penalty herein after mentioned.

And be it further enacted, that if any Negro or Negroes shall refuse to submit to such examinations as is before directed, or after examination, become refractory and unwilling to serve any person or persons to whom, by order and approbation of the said Justices, such Negro or Negroes shall be bound as aforesaid, that then it shall and may be lawful for the said justices to commit such Negro or Negroes to the House of Correction or County Gaol and there keep him or them at hard labour until such time as they consent to be examined or bound as aforesaid....

Provided always, that if any Negro or Negroes shall think him, her, or themselves injured or aggrieved by the proceedings of the Justices, they may complain to the Justices in their General Sessions of the Peace for Relief therein.

DOCUMENT 73:

A Bill Relating to Negroes (Unpassed), New Brunswick, 6 February 1801[6]

Stair Agnew, a Loyalist from Virginia, attempted to enact legislation that would have given statute recognition to slavery. The bill claimed that slavery was legal because of a 1791 Act of Parliament encouraging immigration to His Majesty's colonies. Under Agnew's proposed bill, the children of slave mothers would be enslaved no matter the condition of their fathers (possibly white or free black). Facing stiff opposition, he decided to withdraw the bill.

Whereas in and by an Act of Parliament made in the 30th year of the Reign of his present Majesty instituted—an Act for Encouraging new Settlers in his majesty's colonies and plantations in America, any person, or persons being a Subject or Subjects belonging to the Territories of the United States of America were authorised to bring into any of the Territories belonging to his majesty in North America, any negroes household furniture and other articles Herein mentioned under the Regulations, and Restrictions, in said act contained: And whereas all Sales or Bargains for the sale of any Negro, or other article so imported, which should be made within twelve calendar months after Importation thereof, are by said act declared null and void....

[A]ll Ownership shall be deemed, and computed from the Female, or mother of such child or children whose state and condition shall Regulate....

And be it further enacted that if any person, or persons shall receive, harbour, or conceal any Negro servant, or detain them from the service of their Owner or Master, for the space of __ Hours, every person, or persons, so receiving, harbouring, and concealing, or detaining such Negro servant or servants shall incur the possibility of [no amount given] pounds to be levied by [Distress] and Sale of the Offenders Goods and Chattels upon conviction before any of his Majesty's Justices of the peace.

6 A Bill relating to Negroes, 6 February 1801, Legislative Assembly Records, RS 24, S 14-B 9, PANB. There is another version of this bill: A Bill relating to Negroes [read 1st time—2nd 12 February 1801 + ordered to be committed, 13th February 1801, progress. Withdrawn].

DOCUMENT 74:

AN ACT *to repeal an Act made and passed in the twenty-first year of his late Majesty's reign intituled* "An Act, *declaring that* Baptism of SLAVES *shall not exempt them from* BONDAGE," Prince Edward Island, 1825[7]

This act simply repealed the 1781 Slave Baptism Act (see Document 69, p. 125), making slavery illegal, but it is rather unlikely that there were any slaves in the mid-1820s in Prince Edward Island, but the 1828 Monserrat document indicates that there may have been a few. (See Document 75, p. 133.)

A Bill instituted, an Act made and passed in the twenty-first year of his late Majesty's Reign intituled "An Act, declaring that Baptism of SLAVES shall not exempt them from BONDAGE,"

Whereas by the aforesaid Act Slavery is sanctioned and permitted within this Island and it is highly necessary, that an Act so entirely at variance with the Laws of England and the freedom of the Country should be forthwith repealed, and Slavery forever hereafter abolished in this Colony.

7 AN ACT *to repeal an Act made and passed in the twenty-first year of his late Majesty's reign intituled* "An Act, *declaring that* Baptism *of* SLAVES *shall not exempt them from* BONDAGE," CO 228, Colonial Office Acts, #4, Prince Edward Island, 1812–1829, MS Nos. 181–278, Public Archives of Prince Edward Island.

DOCUMENT 75:

Prince Edward Island and Montserrat Connection, 1828[8]

This document is a reminder of the surprising connections between the West Indies and the Maritimes, especially in terms of slavery. This document highlights that there might have been slaves in Prince Edward Island much later than most historians recognize.

I Matthew William Blake (for Catharine Ormsby) do swear that the Return now by me delivered to be registered contains to the best of my knowledge and belief a true faithful and accurate account and description of all the Slaves belonging to Catharine Ormsby and being within this Island (Save and Except the following Slaves of the Names as follows Charles Male Black Twenty Years, Mary Jane Female Black Thirteen Years, Fanny Female Coloured Eleven Years, Edward Male Black Eight Years, residing with Mr. Ormsby at Prince Edward Island). As Also a true faithful and accurate detail of addition to or deduction from the stock [?] of Slaves in my Possession as aforesaid at the time of making the last preceding return as have since happened together with the particular cause or causes of such addition or deduction. And I do further swear that none of the said Slaves has been to my knowledge imported into this Island contrary to the existing laws for abolishing the Slave Trade.

Sworn to before me
This 13th Decr. 1828

So help me God
M.W. Blake

Jno. Trott, J.P.

8 13 December 1828, Montserrat Slave Register, Kew is T_71_450 page 285, National Archives, UK. Thanks to Mr. Neil How of the Montserrat National Trust, Montserrat, W.I., for sharing this document.

PART V

Wills and Church Records

Wills and church records are vital sources for illuminating relations between individual slaves and their owners. What emerges from wills and probate records are the wide range of relationships between slaves and owners, ranging from cruelty to genuine feelings of affection. Church records can be used to discern the number of slave baptisms or marriages, but they can also include crucial stories like the sad life of Diana Bastian.

DOCUMENT 76:
Will of Joseph Totten, Nova Scotia, 1788[1]

A well-to-do Loyalist from New York, Joseph Totten's will lists five enslaved people of African descent. He gave the three black children away to his daughters, but not the other slaves, which means that a slave family was probably broken up.

In the Name of God Amen. I Joseph Totten of Annapolis Royal in the County of Annapolis and province of Nova Scotia Merchant being weak in body, but of sound Mind, Memory, and understanding: do make and ordain this my last Will and Testament....

I give and bequeath my Negro Girl Slave named Clarinda to my Daughter Phebe Totten ... and To my Daughter Mary Totten I Give and bequeath my Negro Girl Slave named Silvia ... And, I give and bequeath my Negro Girl Slave named Bella [?] to my daughter Jane....

An Account of Property belonging to the Estate of Jos. Totten deceased ... A Lott of Land at the point of the Town of Annapolis Bot. of Mary M. Howe for the Sum of ______£150.0.0
... 1 Negro Boy £50 1 Negro wench £60
3 Children £15 Total £125 New York Money}is £78.2.6

1 Will of Joseph Totten, 1788, Annapolis County, NSA.

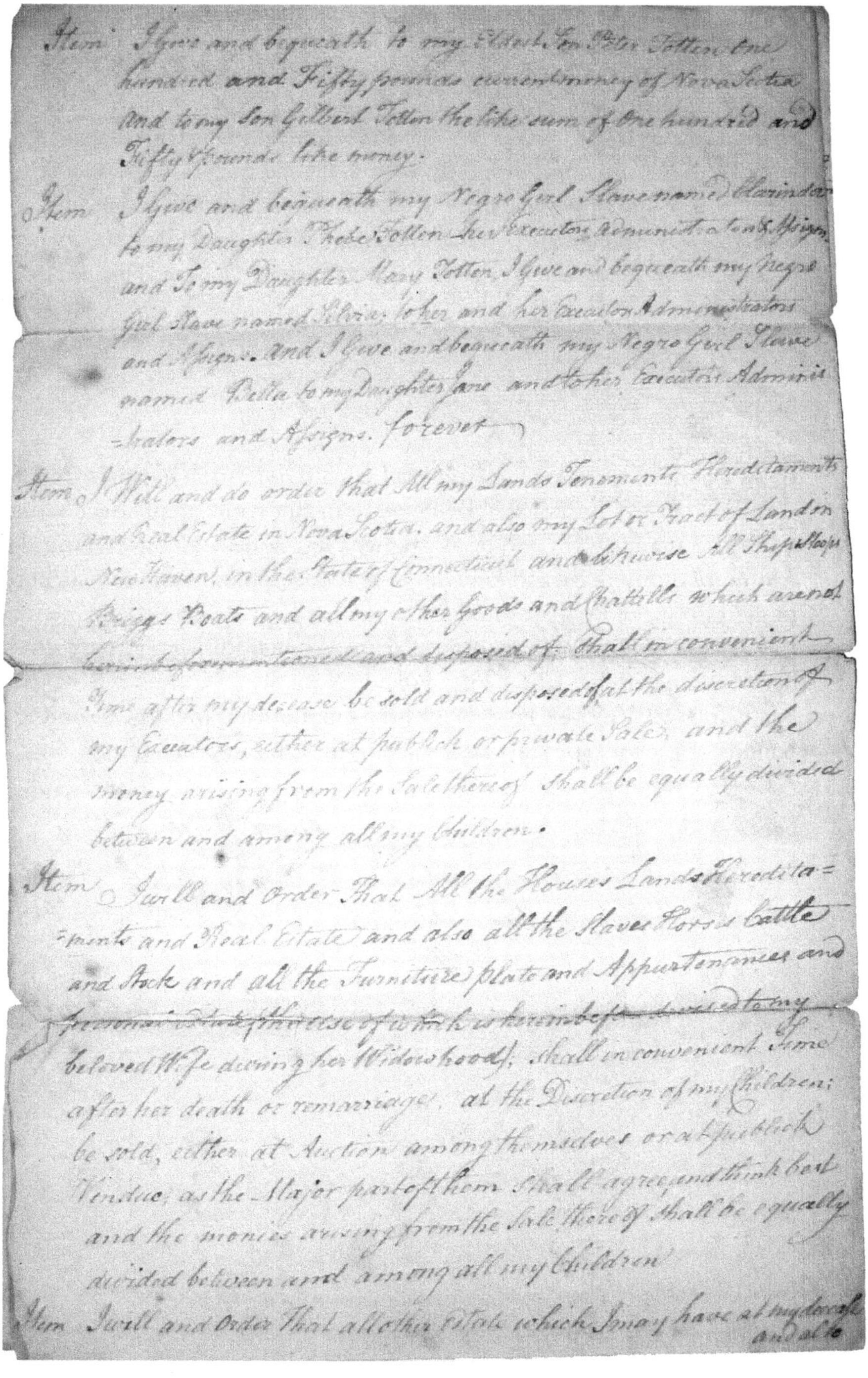

Item I give and bequeath to my Eldest Son Peter Totten One hundred and Fifty pounds current money of Nova Scotia And to my Son Gilbert Totten the like sum of One hundred and Fifty pounds like money.

Item I give and bequeath my Negro Girl Slave named Clarinda to my Daughter Phebe Totten her Executors Administrators and Assigns and To my Daughter Mary Totten I give and bequeath my Negro Girl Slave named Silvia; to her and her Executors Administrators and Assigns. And I give and bequeath my Negro Girl Slave named Bella to my Daughter Jane and to her Executors Adminis-trators and Assigns. forever

Item I Will and do order that All my Lands Tenements Hereditaments and Real Estate in Nova Scotia, and also my Lot or Tract of Land in New Haven, in the State of Connecticut and Likewise All Ships Sloops Briggs Boats and all my other Goods and Chattells which are not ~~herein before mentioned and disposed of~~, Shall in convenient Time after my decease be sold and disposed of at the discretion of my Executors, either at publick or private Sale, and the money arising from the Sale thereof shall be equally divided between and among all my Children.

Item I will and Order That All the Houses Lands Heredita-ments and Real Estate and also all the Slaves Horses Cattle and Stock and all the Furniture plate and Appurtenances and ~~personal Estate the use of which is herein before devised to my~~ beloved Wife during her Widowhood, shall in convenient Time after her death or remarriage, at the Discretion of my Children; be sold, either at Auction among themselves or at publick Vendue, as the Major part of them shall agree, and think best and the monies arising from the Sale there of shall be equally divided between and among all my Children

Item I will and Order That all other Estate which I may have at my decease and also

Will of Joseph Totten of Annapolis, 12 March 1788. Nova Scotia Archives, Annapolis County Probate Records, Estate Case File T1: microfilm 19057.

DOCUMENT 77:
Will of Thomas Leonard, Nova Scotia, 1788[2]

As discussed in the introduction, there were a wide range of interactions between slaves and their owners, which ran the spectrum from acts of cruelty to signs of affection. Some slaves like Diana Bastian (see Document 79, p. 140) suffered immensely, while others might have secured their freedom. In this case, Phillis and her daughter gained their freedom and obtained an important sum of money to help them build a new life.

In the Name of God Amen, I Thomas Leonard of Horton in Kings County and Province of Nova Scotia, Being weak in Body, but of a Perfect Sound mind and memory Blessed be Almighty God same, Calling to mind the Mortality of my Body and knowing that it is Appointed for all men, once to die I do make Publish and declare this my Last Will and Testament.... I Give and Bequeath to my former Negro Woman Phillis [?] I have given her freedom with her Child. Fifty Pounds Nova Scotia Currency to be paid her as follows. Viz. Ten Pounds in three months after my decease and ten pounds a year for four years after making the Said fifty Pounds.

2 Will of Thomas Leonard, Kings County, 1788, NSA.

DOCUMENT 78:
Will of Anna Lillie (or Ann Lilie), Nova Scotia, 1789[3]

A Loyalist widow from Massachusetts, Anna Lillie's husband Theophilus died after the couple arrived in Nova Scotia. Mrs. Lillie clearly cared for her slave, offering him freedom, money, and his comfortable bed to sleep upon. We must remember that during slavery some owners and enslaved individuals held truly affectionate feelings for one another. This should not blind us to other examples of cruelty between masters and slaves. The relationships between slaves and owners were remarkably multifaceted and ran the spectrum from affectionate feelings to depraved cruelty.

In the Name of God Amen. I Ann Lilie of Halifax, Widow considering the uncertainty of this mortal life, and being of sound and perfect mind and memory, do make and publish this my last will and testament, in manner and form following that is to say. First, I give and bequeath all my wearing apparel, and household linen to my relations Mrs. Mary Cox, her daughter, and grand-daughter, and my niece [?] Andrews to be equally divided between them, shared and share alike, and in case of the decease of any or other of them, her portion to be equally divided among the survivors.... It is also my will and intention that my black man Casar be free, and that the Sum of Ten Pounds be retained and left in the hands of my herein after named Executor, to be applied to the use of said Casar, in case of Sickness, or other necessity, at the discretion of my said Executor.... I the aforementioned Anna Lillie do hereby bequeath to my [within?] named black Man Casar the Feather Bed + Bedstead whereupon he usually sleeps, and also the bed clothes and bedding belonging thereto.

3 Will of Anna Lillie, Halifax County, 1789, NSA.

DOCUMENT 79:

Teenage Slave Diana Bastian Burial Note—Her Rape and Pregnancy by George More, Member of Council, Cape Breton, 1792[4]

The church recorder memorialized the sad life of teenager Diana Bastian (her surname has been spelled various ways, Bustian, Bastian, Bestian) in this burial record. His extraordinary account highlights the brutal life of Bastian, but also her refusal to allow George More (who was much older than Bastian) and his powerful friends to dehumanize her.

Sept. 15th 1792

Buried Diana Bastian a Negro Girl belonging to Abraham Cuyler, Esq. in the 15th year of her Age, she was Deluded and Ruined at Government House by George More Esq. the Naval officer and one of Governor Macarmick's Counsel by whom she was pregnant with Twins and delivered [of], but one of them; She most earnestly implored the favour of Mr. More's Brother Justice's to be **admitted to her oath**, concerning her pregnancy by him, but was refused that with every other assistance by him & them.

admitted to her oath: Presumably to give sworn testimony or an affidavit.

4 15 September 1792, Burial Record, St. George's Anglican Church, Sydney: 1785–1827.

DOCUMENT 80:
Will of Caleb Fowler, Nova Scotia, 1793[5]

Originally from New York, Caleb Fowler settled in Annapolis county, Nova Scotia, with his family and slaves (Hannah and her daughter Diana). His will is an example of how slave-owners were more than willing to sell children away from their mothers. Fowler's relatives had unlimited power over Hannah and her daughter. Not surprisingly, there is no mention of Hannah's husband or the father of her child. Perhaps Fowler or one of his relatives fathered Diana. There was no avenue open for Hannah and her child to achieve liberty except to run away. Slaveholding families such as the Fowlers used a combination of coercion, terror, violence, and threats when dealing with slaves who were part of their family.

In the Name of God Amen I Caleb Fowler of the Township of Granville, County of Annapolis and province of Nova Scotia Esquire, being of sound Mind and Memory and thanks be to God for the Calling to mind the mortality of my Body, knowing that it is appointed for all men once to die, do make this my last Will and Testament.... I give [my wife Mary Fowler] my Negro Wench named Hannah to be hers as long as she remains my Widow and no longer. I order and it is my Will that the said Negro Wench Hannah and her Child Diana shall remain in my Family if they are disposed of before my son Caleb is Eighteen years old, then if my Children should wish to keep them, whoever they live with, shall allow a reasonable price for them or either of them, and in case the said Hannah does not behave herself well after my decease, I order her to be sold at the discretion of Executors ... and it is my Will that the said negro child Dianah[6] shall remain with her Mother (if either is sold) until she is ten years old, then one of my said daughters as they two can agree to have her, which ever takes her to allow a reasonable price to be deducted out of their share or Legacy abovementioned for her.

5 Will of Caleb Fowler, 1793, Annapolis County, NSA.

6 Fowler spelled her name differently in two places in this document.

DOCUMENT 81:
Will of George Cornwall, Nova Scotia, 1799[7]

Although some owners freed slaves outright in their wills, others preferred to attach strict and sometimes impossible conditions to the possibility of freedom. This enabled them to maintain control over their slaves, while pretending to make an offer of liberty that could be withdrawn at any time. It might seem that Cornwall's family possessed every advantage in their relationship with their slaves, but in this case such an interpretation oversimplifies the situation. The slaves could feign satisfaction and respect for their owner, while doing just enough to gain their liberty.

In the name of God Amen I George Cornwall of Granville in the County of Annapolis and Province of Nova Scotia Esquire, being in good health and of sound and [?] mind memory and understanding blessed to God for the same, but considering the uncertainty of this life and the certainty of Death do make and publish this my last will and testament.... I give to Charity my beloved wife all my negro slaves requesting her to manumit and set them free by her will after her decease, but in case they do not behave as honest and orderly servants[;] I wish she would sell them, as undeserving of her or my intended bounty towards them.

7 Will of George Cornwall, Annapolis County, 1799, NSA. Charity Cornwall (also spelled Cornwell) owned three slaves in 1807 (see Document 53, p. 93).

DOCUMENT 82:
Will of Jacob Ellegood, New Brunswick, 1802[8]

A native of Virginia, Jacob Ellegood owned several slaves in New Brunswick. He served in the New Brunswick legislative assembly and also owned a large farm. He was the brother-in law of John Saunders who served as Chief Justice of the New Brunswick Supreme Court (also from Virginia). Readers should pay very close attention to the number of slaves mentioned in the will.

This is the last Will & Testament of ... Jacob Ellegood of the county of York in the Province of New Brunswick, Esquire of which will I have caused two parts to be written both of the same tenor words and form....

... And I give and bequeath all my negroes (except one negro wench called Betty which I give to my son William Ellegood and one negro girl not above the age of twelve years which I give to my grand daughter Rebecca Atkinson Ellegood to be chosen by my said grand daughter)....

... And I give to my said dear wife one third part of all my negroes (not herein otherwise disposed of)....

... And I give and bequeath to my said son Jacob Ellegood my negro boy called John and my farming utensils, saddles bridles sleigh and harness and one third part of all my livestock and negroes....

... And I give to my said son John Saunders Ellegood my mulatto wench called Pleasant and her three children James, Sally, and William, and one feather bedding and bedstead.

... And I give and bequeath unto my said son Samuel Inglis Ellegood my negro boy called Irvin and also one third part of all my negroes.

8 Will of Jacob Ellegood, 1802, PANB.

DOCUMENT 83:
Will of Benjamin Belcher, Nova Scotia, 1801[9]

In 1801, Benjamin Belcher owned more slaves than the vast majority of Maritime slaveholders. Indeed, most slaveholders usually owned less than three slaves. There were exceptions to this rule, such as John Polhemus, who owned 10 slaves in Nova Scotia in 1807. Belcher's ownership of seven slaves is still extraordinarily high for Nova Scotia. Belcher seems to have arrived in Nova Scotia in the 1760s, but he was not a New England Planter, coming instead from Gibraltar. In 1797, he received an enormous grant of land (over 6,000 acres) and owned a store in Cornwallis, which was part of the Annapolis region and home to somewhat fertile land. Indeed, this area was home to many of Nova Scotia's slaves after the Loyalist influx in 1783. Belcher's will indicates that he had no intention of freeing his slaves, instead preferring to bequeath them to relatives. This is somewhat surprising because Nova Scotia's judges were slowly ruling against slavery at this time, and some owners were freeing slaves and offering them various forms of indentured servitude.

In the name of God Amen, I Benjamin Belcher of Cornwallis Kings County and Province of Nova Scotia Esquire being in sound health of body and of perfect mind memory blessed be God but considering the great uncertainty of this transitory life do this day and year to wit being the twenty-eight day of March in the year of our Lord and Saviour one Thousand and Eight Hundred and One at Cornwallis aforesaid make and publish this my last Will and Testament in manner following.... I give and bequeath my Negro Woman to my beloved Wife during her lifetime and after her death at her disposal I give and bequeath my Negro Boy called Prince to my son Stephen Belcher during his life after that to his closest surviving son I give my Negro Girl Diana to my daughter Elizabeth Belcher Sheffield and after her death to her eldest heir made of her body [?]. I give my Negro man named Jack and my Negro boy Samuel and Negro boy James and Negro Girl called Chloe to my son Benjamin and his Heirs for ever charging them my children unto whom I have entrusted these Negro people with never to sell barter or exchange them or any of them under any pretension except it is for whose bad [?] Offences as will render them not safe to be kept in the Family and that to be adjudged of by three Justices of the Peace in said

9 Will of Benjamin Belcher, 1801, Kings County, Will Book, vol. 1, 222–27.

Township and in such case as their order they may be sold and disposed of. And I further request as soon as these young Negroes shall be capable to be taught to read, they shall be learnt the word of God.

DOCUMENT 84:
Will of Jacob Troop, Nova Scotia, 1805[10]

In this document, Jacob Troop would have allowed Hannah to remain a slave for another 19 years. Surely Troop knew of the Delancey Decision (1803–04), which limited the rights of slaveholders in Nova Scotia. So the fact that he remained committed to enslaving a young girl for nearly two decades speaks to the fact that he saw slavery lasting for the foreseeable future. At the very same time, every state in New England as well as New York and New Jersey had adopted immediate or gradual emancipation.

In the Name of God Amen

The Twentieth Day of January 1805—I Jacob Troop of Granville Farmer being not well in Body, but of perfect mind and memory, Thanks be given my God ... this my Last will and Testament.... At the Death of my Beloved wife Anna, the Black girl Hannah if [she serves] as a Faithful Servant till she is Thirty years of Age she is then to have her freedom, but if she is not Thirty years of Age at the Death of my Beloved wife Anna, then her service is to be devided equally among my five Daughters till she arrives to the age of Thirty, being now eleven years of age.

10 Will of Jacob Troop, Annapolis County, 1805, NSA.

DOCUMENT 85:
Will of Isaac Bonnell, Nova Scotia, 1806[11]

In this will, Isaac Bonnell clearly expressed some sentimental attachment to his young slaves. He intended to free them and also to provide them with some basic necessities such as clothing. He also wanted them to have a rudimentary understanding of the Bible, because that would help them in early-nineteenth-century society. Nevertheless, these slaves would not gain their freedom until their mid-twenties, which meant that Bonnell's family would continue to benefit from their labour for many years. There is no mention of these slaves' biological parents, which means that they could have died or been sold. We simply do not have enough information to know.

In The Name of God Amen, I Isaac Bonnell of Digby in the county of Annapolis & Province of Nova Scotia.... My Desire is that My Black Boys George, Tom, & Bob—be Taught to Read [?] in the Bible & to write Legible hand & that they be Sett at Liberty as they [?] Arrive to the Age of Twenty four years. Each to be allow'd [?] of good new Cloathes of Every Description Beside their Common wearing apparel. George Was Born in November 1790. Tom Was born in May 1792. And Bob Was Born in February 1794—

11 Will of Isaac Bonnell, Annapolis County, 1806, NSA.

DOCUMENT 86:

Will of William Wanton, New Brunswick, 1812[12]

In this will, a slave-owner decided to give a sum of money to his former slave, which was not unusual for owners who had manumitted slaves and had the financial means to leave a gift.

In the name of God, Amen, I William Wanton of the City of Saint John in the City and County of Saint John in the Province of New Brunswick, Esquire being sick and weak in body but of a sound and disposing mind and memory ... unto my late negro Slave and Servant Buck (to whom I have some time since given his freedom) the sum of one hundred dollars, to be paid to him as soon after my death (if he should so long live) as my dear wife should see fit.

12 Will of William Wanton, 1812, PANB.

DOCUMENT 87:
Will of William Schurman, Prince Edward Island, 1819[13]

Originally from New Rochelle, New York, William Schurman supported the Loyalist cause during the Revolutionary War. In 1783, he left the United States with his family including two slaves and eventually settled in Prince Edward Island. He worked as farmer and businessman, earning a comfortable living. He also served in the colonial legislature. Like most island slave-owners, he came from the elite of society and remained widely respected throughout his life. His will is fascinating because of the way he refers to Susannah as a member of the family. This wording was common especially in New England and the Maritimes, where slaves lived in close contact with their enslavers. Clearly, Schurman felt some affection for Susannah in offering her lifetime support or 50 pounds if she wished to strike out on her own. The document illuminates the bonds of affection between some slaves and their owners. Lastly, readers should recognize the term "servant" that William used to describe Susannah. In all likelihood, she had been a slave for many years, but eventually William freed her and she continued on with the family as a domestic servant. In 1819, slavery remained legal in PEI and would not be outlawed for another six years.

In the Name of God Amen, I William Schurman of Bedeque, Farmer in Prince County Prince Edward Island being of sound mind, memory, and understanding do make this my last will and Testament in manner following, that is to say, I desire my body may be buried in the burying ground at Bedeque near the Church with as little Expense as decency will permit and that all of my debts and funeral expenses be paid as soon after my decease.... And also my desire and will is that my Negro servant Susannah Schurman shall be provided for in the family as long as she wishes to remain in the family with meat drink and clothing as long as she lives, but if it be her choice to leave the family my will is to give her fifty pounds lawful money of this Island to be raised out of my Estate.

13 Will of William Schurman, 1819, RG 62, ser. I, lib. I, fol. 130, PAROPEI.

SUGGESTED READINGS

The study of slavery in Canada has grown tremendously in the last 30 years. See the excellent work of the following scholars:

Bell, D.G. "Slavery and the Judges of Loyalist New Brunswick," *University of New Brunswick Law Journal* 31 (1982): 9–42.

Cahill, Barry. "Habeas Corpus and Slavery in Nova Scotia: *R v. Hecht, ex parte Rachel*, 1798," *University of New Brunswick Law Journal* 44 (1995): 179–209.

Cahill, Barry. "Slavery and the Judges of Loyalist Nova Scotia," *University of New Brunswick Law Journal* 43 (1994): 73–135.

Cooper, Afua. *The Hanging of Angélique: The Untold Story of Slavery in Canada and the Burning of Old Montréal* (Athens: U of Georgia P, 2007).

Cottreau-Robins, Catherine. "Searching for the Enslaved in Nova Scotia's Loyalist Landscape," *Acadiensis* 43 (Winter/Spring 2014): 125–36.

Cottreau-Robins, Catherine. "The Loyalist Plantation: An Interdisciplinary Approach to Early African-Nova Scotian Settlement," *Journal of the Royal Nova Scotia Historical Society* 17 (2014): 32–56.

Donovan, Kenneth. "Female Slaves as Sexual Victims in Île Royale," *Acadiensis* 43 (Winter/Spring 2014): 147–56.

Donovan, Kenneth. "Slaves in Île Royale, 1713–1758," *French Colonial History* 5 (2004): 25–42.

Donovan, Kenneth. "A Nominal List of Slaves and Their Owners in Île Royale, 1713–1760," *Nova Scotia Historical Review* 16 (1996): 151–62.

Donovan, Kenneth. "Slaves and Their Owners in Île Royale, 1713–1760," *Acadiensis* 25 (Autumn 1995): 3–32.

Harris, Jennifer. "Black Life in a Nineteenth Century New Brunswick Town," *Journal of Canadian Studies* 46, 1 (Winter 2012): 138–66.

Mackey, Frank. *Done with Slavery: The Black Fact in Montreal, 1760–1840* (Montreal-Kingston: McGill-Queen's UP, 2010).

MacLeod-Leslie, Heather. "Archaeology and Atlantic Canada's African Diaspora," *Acadiensis* 43 (Winter/Spring 2014): 137–45.

Nelson, Charmaine. *Slavery, Geography and Empire in Nineteenth-Century Marine Landscapes of Montreal and Jamaica* (New York: Routledge, 2017).

Robertson, Allen. "Bondage and Freedom: Apprentices, Servants and Slaves in Colonial Nova Scotia," *Collections of the Royal Nova Scotia Historical Society* 44 (1996): 57–69.

Rushforth, Brett. *Bonds of Alliance: Indigenous and Atlantic Slaveries in New France* (Chapel Hill: U of North Carolina P, 2012).

Troxler, Carole Watterson. "Re-enslavement of Black Loyalists: Mary Postell in South Carolina, East Florida, and Nova Scotia," *Acadiensis* 37 (Summer/Fall, 2008): 70–85.

Trudel, Marcel. *L'esclavage au Canada français: Histoire et conditions de l'esclavage* (Quebec: Presses Universitaires Laval, 1960).

Whitfield, Harvey Amani. "The African Diaspora in Atlantic Canada: History, Historians, and Historiography," *Acadiensis* 46 (Winter/Spring 2017): 213–32.

Whitfield, Harvey Amani. *North to Bondage: Loyalist Slavery in the Maritimes* (Vancouver: U of British Columbia P, 2016).

Whitfield, Harvey Amani. "The Struggle over Slavery in the Maritime Colonies," *Acadiensis* 41 (Summer/Autumn 2012): 17–44.

Whitfield, Harvey Amani. "Slavery in English Nova Scotia," *Journal of the Royal Nova Scotia Historical Society* 13 (2010): 23–40.

Whitfield, Harvey Amani. "Black Loyalists and Black Slaves in Maritime Canada," *History Compass* 5 (2007): 1980–97.

Whitfield, Harvey Amani, and Barry Cahill. "Slave Life and Slave Law in Colonial Prince Edward Island, 1769–1825," *Acadiensis* 38 (Summer/Autumn 2009): 29–51.

Wigmore, Gregory. "Before the Railroad: From Slavery to Freedom in the Canadian-American Borderland," *Journal of American History* 98 (September 2011): 437–54.

Winks, Robin W. *The Blacks in Canada: A History* (New Haven: Yale UP, 1971).

From the Publisher

A name never says it all, but the word "Broadview" expresses a good deal of the philosophy behind our company. We are open to a broad range of academic approaches and political viewpoints. We pay attention to the broad impact book publishing and book printing has in the wider world; for some years now we have used 100% recycled paper for most titles. Our publishing program is internationally oriented and broad-ranging. Our individual titles often appeal to a broad readership too; many are of interest as much to general readers as to academics and students.

Founded in 1985, Broadview remains a fully independent company owned by its shareholders—not an imprint or subsidiary of a larger multinational.

For the most accurate information on our books (including information on pricing, editions, and formats) please visit our website at www.broadviewpress.com. Our print books and ebooks are available for sale on our site.

broadview press

www.broadviewpress.com

This book is made of paper from well-managed FSC® - certified forests, recycled materials, and other controlled sources.

MIX
Paper from responsible sources
FSC® C103567

PCF

BIO GAS ENERGY

PERMANENT